Understanding
Zora Neale Hurston's
Their Eyes Were
Watching God

The Greenwood Press "Literature in Context" Series
Student Casebooks to Issues, Sources, and Historical Documents

UNDERSTANDING
Zora Neale Hurston's
Their Eyes Were Watching God

A STUDENT CASEBOOK TO ISSUES, SOURCES, AND HISTORICAL DOCUMENTS

Neal A. Lester

The Greenwood Press
"Literature in Context" Series
Claudia Durst Johnson, Series Editor

G P

GREENWOOD PRESS
Westport, Connecticut • London

Library of Congress Cataloging-in-Publication Data

Lester, Neal A.
    Understanding Zora Neale Hurston's Their eyes were watching God :
a student casebook to issues, sources, and historical documents /
Neal A. Lester.
        p.   cm.—(The Greenwood Press "Literature in context"
series, ISSN 1074–598X)
    Includes bibliographical references and index.
    ISBN 0–313–30210–3 (alk. paper)
    1. Hurston, Zora Neale.   Their eyes were watching God.   2. Afro-
Americans—Florida—Social life and customs—Sources.   3. Afro-
Americans—Florida—Folklore—Sources.   4. Afro-American women in
literature.   5. Florida—Race relations—Sources.   I. Title.
II. Series.
PS3515.U789T638   1999
813'.52—dc21   98–55342

British Library Cataloguing in Publication Data is available.

Library of Congress Catalog Card Number: 98–55342
ISBN: 0–313–30210–3
ISSN: 1074–598X

First published in 1999

Greenwood Press, 88 Post Road West, Westport, CT 06881
An imprint of Greenwood Publishing Group, Inc.
www.greenwood.com

Printed in the United States of America

The paper used in this book complies with the
Permanent Paper Standard issued by the National
Information Standards Organization (Z39.48–1984).

10 9 8 7 6 5 4 3 2 1

Contents

Acknowledgments

I am indebted to Claudia D. Johnson for encouraging me to share my thoughts on Zora Neale Hurston in this forum and with a broader audience. I am also much indebted to my Mom, Dad, Granny, and other extended family who enriched my life as a child in the South through community rituals I am only now able to appreciate fully and luxuriate in. My very special appreciation is extended to my research assistant, Papatya Bucak, for her steadfast commitment, dedication, punctuality, and careful eye for details. Finally, this project would not have been completed without the unyielding patience and understanding of my wife, Adelina, and my children, Jasmine and Jared.

Introduction

Zora Neale Hurston's *Their Eyes Were Watching God* (1937) is now a standard text in American literature, African American literature, and women's studies courses from high school to graduate school. The popularity of Hurston's novel is largely due to the groundbreaking efforts of writer Alice Walker in the early 1970s to resurrect Hurston (1903–1960) and her work from literary and critical oblivion. To rediscover and to reintroduce Hurston was, according to Walker, to celebrate and legitimize the diversity and textured nuances of African American culture—language, folklore, American political and social history, American race relations, feminism and womanism; in short, to provide readers today with an exploration into the complex life of a black woman artist whose prolific works and whose enigmatic life defy categorization within others' convenient boundaries.[1] Many other writers of the Harlem Renaissance described the experiences of southern blacks who migrated north for safety from lynching and other violent acts and for more economic and educational opportunities. Countee Cullen writes of northern travel in "Incident" (1925); Jean Toomer writes of the exciting nightlife in "Seventh Street" (*Cane* 1923); Langston Hughes's character Jesse B. Semple shares his life through storytelling in a Harlem bar (*The Best of Simple* 1961); and Nella Larsen explores the entanglements of racial and sexual passing [feigning a reality perceived as socially advantageous] among upper-middle-class African Americans (*Passing* 1929).

Their Eyes Were Watching God appeared at the tail end of what is termed in American literature as the Harlem Renaissance. Roughly between 1917—the end of World War I—and the 1930 stock market crash that marked the beginning of the Great Depression, throngs of southern African Americans migrated north—a migration that technically began as early as 1910—primarily to the northeast for economic and social reasons, escaping more overt and often violent manifestations of tensed black-white race relations. A time when "the Negro was in vogue," this was a time of cultural celebration of blackness—black visual arts, black music, black intellectual thought, black performing arts, and black identity. Leading voices of the Harlem Renaissance challenged black authors and artists to define African American life beyond the prescribed boundaries of stereotype and caricature, sentimentality, and social assimilation. Arguably a movement among intellectuals, the Harlem Renaissance proved spiritually and aesthetically liberating for African Americans and established global connections with an African past. Hurston's emphasis on rural common folk of the south both challenged and continued some of the fundamental tenants of the Harlem Renaissance: national and global community, self-determination, and race pride. The most concentrated place of this cultural explosion was Harlem (New York).

Despite the fact that Hurston is a staple in many African American literature and women's studies courses throughout the world, Hurston, the person, was and remains an enigma to scholars and students. For one, while her gravestone marker states that Hurston was born in 1901, other sources claim her birth in 1891 or 1903. Scholars looking closely at her family history records have fairly definitively concluded that 1891 is the more accurate date. Born in Nostasulga, Alabama, Hurston grew up in the all-colored town of Eatonville, Florida, about ten miles northeast of Orlando and the source of much of her folklore writings about African American culture. The daughter of a Baptist preacher and three-time mayor of Eatonville, Hurston had a rather strained relationship with her father but a closer one with her mother. Perhaps from these relationships with her own parents Hurston drew upon certain domestic relationships that play out in her fiction.

As a child, Hurston was spirited and rebellious, and this persona developed eccentrically in her adult relations. Hurston was a prankster, believed to have had a magnetic personality that simultaneously charmed and puzzled people. She was a nonconformist who confused many about her own public and private racial and sexual politics. For readers then and now, her writings furthered that ambiguity of her political and personal positions. From showing up at parties dressed in Mammy costume and "borrowing" change from a beggar's cup, to her relationship—both public and private—with her white female benefactor, Hurston's persona was for some as invitingly ambiguous as her fictive tales about the complexities of African American experience.

Hurston, schooled in the north at both Barnard College and Howard University, turned south and homeward to Eatonville, Florida, to record the richness of life of those blacks who remained in the south. Hurston's determination to celebrate the survival of a culture and a people in the face of almost insurmountable social, political, and economic odds puts her works at the forefront of discussions of black nationalism, feminism, and womanism.

Published in 1937, Hurston's most popular novel, *Their Eyes Were Watching God*, was not immediately popular. In fact, the novel was largely ignored and greatly criticized by her black male contemporaries, because it allegedly presents blacks in stereotypical ways that white readers enjoyed and encouraged of black writers. This criticism was especially harsh from those who thought that Hurston should be writing more overtly protest pieces about whites as blacks' enemies. While Hurston does not center around white people in the novel, their Jim Crow presence is apparent from the opening through the closing pages. The novel was out of print some thirty years after its initial publication. In 1971, it was reprinted but again out of print by 1975. In 1977, Hurston's novel topped reading lists among American colleges and universities and continues that top billing even today.

Any study of Hurston's novels, short stories, essays, plays, and collected tales reveals the creative genius of one committed to documenting and legitimizing experiences of black people and of black women that had been ignored by white mainstream and patriarchal American society or oversimplified, particularly the experiences of unschooled blacks. *Their Eyes Were Watching God*, published by J. B. Lippincott Company in 1937, is perhaps the single Hurston text that serves as an encyclopedia of African American culture—female sexuality, interracism and intraracism, orality and storytelling rituals, music, communal identities—with a poignant statement on the complexities of the human condition.

Their Eyes Were Watching God is the story of Janie, a black woman of mulatto ancestry, in search of spiritual liberation from patriarchal control. The format of the book is Janie's telling of her own story in her own voice as she remembers the details of her own life. As the storyteller, Janie has an authority that even the readers cannot challenge when they want details, particularly technical details, that Janie does not remember or choose to share. While Janie's story is on many levels gender and racially specific— we never forget that Janie's grandmother was a slave or that the characters arc living during Jim Crow segregation of the 1930s and 1940s—much of Janie's social disruption within the community of black people is gender related. Her intracommunal attacks are largely based on others' opinions of what a woman and especially a woman her age should and should not be doing. Moreover, Janie's story is one of a person who is able to self-define and to transcend restrictive boundaries ultimately through communal storytelling rituals.

Janie's story of resistance begins with her Granny's command that she marry Logan Killicks, a man with a mule and land, to prevent her from throwing her life away now that she has moved into womanhood physiologically. Nanny's great worry, and the catalyst for Janie's search to find marriage in a male partner, is that Janie experiences sexual pleasure under a pear tree and then defines "marriage" through what she witnesses between bees pollinating flowers. That search takes her through two husbands, the old and unattractive Logan, who threatens her repeatedly with violence when she refuses to obey his commands, and the city builder and economically privileged Jody Starks, who wants to mold Janie into his vision of "the Mayor's wife"—one who speaks only when spoken to, dresses as he designs, and stays inside his store as he demands. While Janie waited for love that never came with Logan, her relationship with Jody is initially based on the spiritual and the physical until Jody makes it publicly and privately clear that he plans to mold Janie into his perfect wife. After Jody's physical death, Janie meets and weds Tea Cake Woods, a man significantly younger than she and with absolutely nothing to offer Janie materialistically or financially. Though short-lived, Janie's relationship with Tea Cake allows her to experience the feeling she recalls from the pear tree of her youth. As the hands of fate would have it, the relationship between Janie and Tea Cake ends tragically, and Janie is left with a spiritual excitement at having loved despite her great loss. Through Janie's story, Hurston introduces a number of significant themes that bear out the complexities of human experience: gender roles in marriage, definitions of marriage legally and spiritually, community performance rituals, individual and community storytelling, male and female power struggles, and discrimination within black communities based on skin complexion and hair lengths and textures.

Arguably, Hurston's novel is less about action than the narrative telling of the story that defines the main character Janie as a woman and as a black woman. It defines the collective character of African Americans able to define and empower themselves in racist America through talking.

As with any study of Zora Neale Hurston, this one begins with questions that have no "right" answers. The fact that Hurston's work cannot readily be placed within one particular cultural and social context may explain what brings scholars, students, and teachers to her writing again and again with excitement and freshness and a sense of discovering and celebrating what seems all too familiar and nothing short of complex.

Our examination will address certain fundamental issues that ground the novel:

What are Hurston's attitudes toward black people who lived on the "other side of the creek"?

Are Hurston's portrayals of these "unrefined" and uneducated folk a celebration or a mockery?

Is Hurston's consistent use of southern black dialect far removed from white minstrelsy and its presentation of blacks as unintelligent and blundering?

Does Hurston glorify white people, particularly her white patrons, by catering to their racist notions of how and what fiction about blacks should be written?

Does Hurston oversimplify the oppressions of blacks and women in a racist, sexist, and capitalist American society?

What was Hurston's relation to her Harlem Renaissance contemporaries?

To what extent does Hurston foreground social protest in her work?

To what extent does Hurston simultaneously attack and celebrate black communal rituals?

Does Hurston's presentation of women directly and/or indirectly bash men?

What is the value of Hurston's recycling of folklore materials?

Does Hurston perpetuate an essentialist view [a view that presents black identity without diversity and individual variation] of black identity?

Does Hurston's presentation of relationships between women and men take a secondary position to black-white race relations in her work?

How does language define African American cultural identity, individually and communally?

What is the role of history in Hurston's presentation of race and gender dimensions in the novel?

This casebook is divided into five chapters. Chapter 1 offers a literary analysis of the novel that includes a discussion of the plot, characters, and prevailing themes. Chapter 2 focuses on Hurston's use of language in the novel; it explains the significance of talking and of speech historically, socially, and politically for African Americans and women who were denied this fundamental right by white mainstream America. Chapter 3 discusses issues related to Hurston's presentation of men and women in the novel and centers on female sexuality and domestic violence. Chapter 4 discusses black-white race relations in the novel and considers definitions of blackness and manifestations of black identity. It also offers documents that situate Hurston's hometown of Eatonville, Florida, in a contemporary setting and shows the ways in which Hurston's legacy defines this place in literary and cultural American history. Chapter 5 places the novel within the cultural and aesthetic context of blues music, an American folk music genre. Each chapter concludes with a series of discussion questions or questions for written explorations, followed by bibliographic references for further reading.

Because this casebook recognizes the interdisciplinary nature of literary study, particularly about African American culture and Afrocentric perspectives that do not separate life experiences into neat categories, several kinds of documents are presented here to contextualize Hurston's novel and to ground our exploration: photographs, a minstrel song, an advertisement, an original rap lyric, folktales, newspaper articles, sermons and a prayer, glossaries, public segregation signs, interviews, a literary article, and an excerpt from a book review. To demonstrate the depth and scope of *Their Eyes Were Watching God* aesthetically and culturally, it is important and necessary to engage music, song, religion, history, and popular culture. These documents underscore the timelessness of Hurston's focus on the complex talking rituals that define African American identity and culture. In particular, the documents show how it is impossible to separate past and present, as well as high and low culture, in *Their Eyes Were Watching God*.[2]

NOTES

1. Alice Walker, "Zora Neale Hurston: A Cautionary Tale and a Partisan View," "Looking for Zora," In *In Search of Our Mothers' Gardens: Womanist Prose* (San Diego: Harcourt Brace Jovanovich, 1983).

2. Subsequent references to this novel and edition—University of Illinois Press, 1978—are cited parenthetically in this casebook as *TEWWG* with page number.

Understanding
Zora Neale Hurston's
*Their Eyes Were
Watching God*

1

Literary Analysis

According to a December 1990 survey on "Ethnic Images" conducted by the National Opinion Research Center of the University of Chicago, the majority of respondents—both white and non-white—believe that "blacks are more likely [than whites] to be lazy, violence prone, less intelligent, and less patriotic." Respondents also felt that blacks, more so than whites, "prefer to live on welfare."[1] However progressive our contemporary American society considers itself in terms of effective and open communications and diverse life experiences, preconceived notions of African Americans persist. As narrator Esther Rolle asserts in the documentary film *Ethnic Notions: Black Images in White Minds* (1987), images of blacks being lazy, violence prone, shiftless, untrustworthy, unintelligible, and unintelligent are historically embodied in negative and offensive character representations:

> The mammy . . . the pickaninny . . . the coon . . . the sambo . . . the uncle: well into the middle of the twentieth century, these were some of the most popular depictions of black Americans. . . . [I]mages like these permeated American culture. These were the images that decorated our homes, they served and amused and made us laugh. Taken for granted, they worked their way into the mainstream of American life. Of ethnic caricatures in America, these

have been the most enduring. Today, there's little doubt that they shaped the most gut-level feelings about race.[2]

In his essay entitled "Negro Character as Seen by White Authors" (1933), Sterling A. Brown lists seven distinct character types that define the African American presence in American literature: the contented slave, the wretched freeman (former slave), the comic Negro, the brute Negro, the tragic mulatto (person of mixed race), the local color Negro, and the exotic primitive. Brown lamented that the representation of African Americans in the works of white authors lacked authenticity and reality, insisting that the political and social circumstances of race relations and history made it easier for authors to present comfort with the Other rather than truth about the Other. Brown's bold challenge was made to African American authors: "It is likely that, in spite of the willingness of some Negro authors to accept at face value some of these stereotypes, the exploration of Negro life and character rather than its exploitation must come from Negro authors themselves."[3] Years later, literary theorist and cultural critic Henry Louis Gates Jr. maintains that these character types are common in today's representations of African Americans on television:

> Brown's list of black stereotypes in American literature proves quite serviceable as a guide to the images TV has purveyed for the last two decades. Were we writing a new sitcom using these character types, our cast might look like this—contented slave: Andy, Fred Sanford, J. J. ("Good Times"); wretched freeman: George Jefferson; comic Negro: Flip Wilson; brute Negro: Mr. T ("The A-Team"), Hawk ("Spencer: For Hire"); tragic mulatto: "Julia," Elvin ("Cosby"), Whitley ("A Different World"); local color Negro: Meshach Taylor ("Designing Women"); exotic primitive: Link ("Mod Squad" 1968–1973), most black characters on MTV. If we add the category of Noble Negro (Cliff Huxtable, Benson), our list would be complete.[4]

Brown echoed Alain Locke's essay, "The New Negro" (1992), when he urged African American authors to embrace the complexities of African American identity in their art forms. Locke argued:

> [F]or generations in the mind of America, the Negro has been more of a formula than a human being—a something to be argued about,

condemned or defended, to be "kept down," or "in his place," or "helped up," to be worried with or worried over, harassed or patronized, a social bogey or a burden. The thinking Negro even has been induced to share this same general attitude, to focus his attention on controversial issues, to see himself in the distorted perspective of a social problem.[5]

Locke urged his contemporaries to abandon social imitation, social intimidation, sentimentalism, stereotypes, and caricatures of themselves to create a new Negro with a new attitude about himself and his possibilities. Calling for a spiritual emancipation amid the great migrations (in the 1920s) of rural southern blacks to the northern cities for economic, educational, and more socially safe opportunities, Locke encouraged among his contemporaries a cultural and spiritual self-assertiveness, race consciousness, and self-defensiveness. While attempting to define an ideal of African American representation, Locke established the urgency of African American self-determination and a bold nationalist consciousness.

Zora Neale Hurston's decision to define black nationalist consciousness differently from the social protest of her contemporary, Richard Wright—who presents violence between blacks and whites as a central focus and who centers black men's experiences in a racist society—created much controversy. This was especially significant as some of Hurston's critics regarded her work as performing aesthetically and personally for white patrons at the expense of presenting African American cultural authenticity. In his critique of *Their Eyes Were Watching God*, Wright maintained:

Miss Hurston can write; but her prose is cloaked in that facile sensuality that has dogged Negro expression since the days of Phillis Wheatley. Her dialogue manages to catch the psychological movements of the Negro folk-mind in their pure simplicity, but that's as far as it goes.

Miss Hurston *voluntarily* continues in her novel the tradition which was *forced* upon the Negro in the theater, that is, the minstrel technique that makes the "white folks" laugh. Her characters eat and laugh and cry and work and kill; they swing like a pendulum eternally in the safe and narrow orbit in which America likes to see the Negro live: between laughter and tears.[6]

Although Alain Locke challenged Negro authors and artists to create a new race consciousness that demonstrated complexity of thought, reconceptualization of an African past, and communal celebration, he nevertheless attacked Hurston's novel as "oversimplification," full of "these pseudo-primitives whom the [white] reading public still loves to laugh with, weep over and envy."[7] It is precisely this redefinition of African American social protest and African American identity that Hurston presents in *Their Eyes Were Watching God*. Through an exploration of life and death, romance, family relations, violence, and laughter, Hurston raises the folklore and folk art of African Americans to high culture.

Published in 1937, Zora Neale Hurston's *Their Eyes Were Watching God* is a heterosexual love story textured by a general feminist consciousness and a distinctly African American consciousness. It is the story of Janie, who longs to exert herself as a free, thinking woman in a society of men and women bent on defining *her* realities in *their* selfish terms. Janie's is not a quest for self-identity but rather a journey toward freedom to be herself and to accept responsibility for the choices she makes in search of physical and spiritual self-satisfaction. As Janie tells her story, Hurston celebrates the life of a black woman who is able to accept what she cannot control or understand. While Janie is exalted in Hurston's eyes for her experiential wisdom, Janie herself is humbled by her life experiences, especially the death of Tea Cake, her third and youngest husband, ultimately at her own hand.

Janie first endeavors to appease her grandmother, whose ideas about black women leave Janie no room for independent thought or action. Nanny can only see Janie's emotional and psychological maturity through her own experiences as a former slave controlled by white men. According to Nanny, a black woman ought to want a man with property and the ability to provide for her—hence Nanny's arrangement of Janie's marriage to an older man, Logan Killicks. Bent on making Janie a fieldhand or work animal, when Janie does not obey his demands and commands Logan presents himself in behavior and word like a slave master with insults and threats of violence.

Janie's relationship with Jody Starks is initially one of intense romance, full of rhyme and rhythm. Jody, seemingly very different from Janie's first husband, Logan, is a businessman intent on creating a community of black folk under his official guidance and charge. A man with money, power, and organizational skills, Jody seeks to place Janie atop a pedestal as the mayor's wife without any concern for her wants or needs. For Jody, Janie's role is to move according to his direction and to speak according to his script, one that centers him and seeks to publicly silence Janie. While Janie's resistance to Logan is vocal and ultimately results in her decision to abandon him, her resistance to Jody's dominance and rules is internal and thoughtful. That ultimate defiance comes when she challenges and insults his manhood before an audience of his male peers. His death after twenty years of marriage to Janie almost immediately follows his public embarrassment.

In the beginning of Janie's third romance, Tea Cake—fifteen years younger than Janie—seems her ideal companion. He allows her freedom to experience life as she sees fit without feeling intimidated. As Janie and Tea Cake live as partners and soulmates participating in life harmoniously, their relationship is the envy and curiosity of gossipers and onlookers. They fish, go to baseball games, play checkers, cook meals together. He even teaches her how to shoot a gun. The nosy intraracist, Mrs. Turner, tries to pull Janie away from the "too dark" Tea Cake to consider a romance with her brother. Janie resists the temptation as Tea Cake is all she has ever wanted. In fact, her intense passion for Tea Cake leads her to battle Nunkie, who is allegedly trying to romance Tea Cake. Janie's life with Tea Cake becomes an emotional rollercoaster. He takes her money and stays out all night, then comes home with few or no explanations for his actions. He even hits Janie to signal for curious onlookers and for himself his own constructed masculinity. Yet the depth of Janie's love for Tea Cake sustains her through these moments of emotional duress, for Tea Cake has made her feel the vulnerabilities of love and passion, something she never experienced meaningfully with her two previous husbands. Tea Cake's sickness and subsequent death remind Janie of the precious nature of life and of the dignity necessary to accept what cannot be explained or controlled. As Janie reflects on her experiences in her testimony to her best friend, Phoeby, she does so without regret of love lost but with integrity and strength from love experienced.

Dealing with romance, community rituals, race relations, women's identity, women's sexuality, and individual and communal performance rituals, *Their Eyes Were Watching God* celebrates the complexities of African American people generally and of African American women specifically—complexities denied them historically, politically, and in American fiction. Despite claims that Hurston betrayed black people by presenting them laughing and talking about nothing, the loud claims and critiques of many of her black contemporaries, she presents in *Their Eyes Were Watching God* a storehouse of black cultural wealth—language, rituals, rhymes, rhythms, celebrations, and sufferings—allowing black people fuller existences than white authors typically allowed.

In addition to sexuality and gender roles, Hurston offers a number of thematic ideas related to African American women's independence and romance. Directly connected with the romance is Hurston's fairy tale language, which conjures images of magic and wonder and even surrealism. Jody speaks to Janie first in "rhymes," shiftless Johnny Taylor is doused with fairy dust after Janie's autoerotic experience under the pear tree, and Tea Cake has "de keys tuh de kingdom." Hers is the language of dream, fantasy, and possibility. Even when the reader's more critical eyes and ears want to know if Janie married these men legally and then legally divorced them, Hurston's intent is to allow Janie the authority to tell her story as she remembers it or chooses to remember it.

Hurston's use of nature and nature imagery is also fundamental to the novel. Not only is the hurricane at the novel's end an important vehicle of the plot, but nature generally—trees, birds and bees, flowers—creates a setting in which dream and fantasy can be nourished. The flood, the hurricane, the muck, the outside settings with trees and blooming flowers being pollinated by bees—all reiterate a closeness to the earth and a natural instinct associated with Janie. Images of the sun and horizon give Janie's story epic proportions at the same time the tale grounds Janie and her experiences in the real, the common, and the very possible.

Violence is complexly presented by Hurston as well. From the physical violence of Leafy's rape by the schoolteacher, to the historical rape of slave women by their masters and the threats of violence from Nanny and Janie's three male companions, Hurston shows how basic violence is to human interactions. She also shows that violence results from all kinds of human emotions and motives. Perhaps it is the novel's final moment of violence—the shooting of Tea Cake by Janie—that further demonstrates the uncertainties of life and the ambiguity of experience.

Broader issues covered in the novel include the subjectivity of truth and how human beings arrive at what is true for them individually and spiritually. As Janie tells her story, it becomes others' stories and those of people who have negatively or positively influenced her life. Hurston's ability to merge the aesthetics of orality and literacy attest to the value of language and speech in creating, legitimizing, documenting, and sustaining African American culture.

MINSTRELS

American literary history reveals that African Americans were the subject of American theater long before they were allowed to become participants or performers in that theater. As early as 1769, a white man appeared costumed as a slave in a New York comic opera. In 1799, a white actor appeared in a Boston performance with a black grease painted face to portray "a negro boy." T. D. Rice, in 1836, introduced the character of Jim Crow to the stage, based on a crippled and tattered slave whom Rice imitated with exaggerated self-mocking gestures and mannerisms, and nonsensical rhythmless speech. The character was phenomenally popular among northern white audiences. In the south, Dan Emmett, author of the famous allegedly patriotic southern Confederacy tune, "Dixie, or Dixie Land" (1959)—itself a minstrel song—founded the Virginia Minstrels in 1842. Prior to the publication of Harriet Beecher Stowe's popular and sentimental *Uncle Tom's Cabin* (1852), minstrel shows provided the basis of many white northerners' perceptions of black Americans. By the 1850s, blacks had blackened their already dark faces with grease paint or other makeup and taken to the stage to entertain white audiences with self-mocking and baffoonish exaggerations and language. Always grinning, laughing, wall-eyed and wide lipped, minstrels were a popular American entertainment until the 1890s.

Because of Hurston's use of southern black vernacular—considered the "street talk" of the illiterate common folk—in *Their Eyes Were Watching God* and because her characters participate and luxuriate in a life not centrally focused on all-consuming combat with white racism, many of Hurston's critics felt that her folk characters were akin to minstrels. Her presentation was believed to satisfy white audiences' racist views of blacks as silly, simple, carefree, and unburdened by the complexities of white peoples' lives. On the contrary, Hurston's characters are not self-mocking, and their language is full of figurative nuances that demonstrate a very sophisticated form of storytelling and communicating. Comparing Hurston's characters' textured even lyrical language and the awkward and irregular rhythmed language of the *Uncle Remus Tales* by Joel Chandler Harris (1848–1908) further highlights Hurston's skill at capturing and re-creating the most subtle of linguistic cadences, textures and rituals that largely define African American culture and African American identity.

Minstrel songs were written by whites who were imitating the alleged intellectual and linguistic inferiority of blacks unable to master "standard" English. Minstrel songs—very different from spirituals, work songs, and plantation songs—used grossly exaggerated dialect and offensive language that was awkwardly rhythmed and nonsensical. Because of the popularity of minstrel songs in American culture during the late 1800s, a few blacks authored them as well. Gussie L. Davis (1863–1899), for instance, wrote the popular tune "When They Straighten All the Colored People's Hair" (1894), which mocked the perceived unattractiveness of black people's "nappy" hair.

The following anonymously authored minstrel song, "De History Ob De World (Walk In De Parlor)," appears in Albert E. Wier's edited collection *Songs of the Sunny South* (New York: Appleton and Company, 1929). The volume includes plantation and minstrel ditties, negro spirituals, and Stephen Foster's—also an author of minstrel songs such as "Uncle Ned"—ballads and songs. Among the minstrel songs included in the collection and labeled as such are popular Disney tunes "Jimmy Crack Corn" and "Oh! Susanna."

"De History Ob De World" is a mocking variation on the Creation myth. Compare the language of this minstrel song with that of a tale from an Uncle Remus collection, then compare both to the textured language Hurston uses in her fiction. How are the versions of black vernacular different?

The picture of two male minstrels—blacks in blackface, which is a type of theater makeup to portray black skin—appeared on the cover of a brochure advertising director Marlon Riggs's award-

De History Ob De World
(Walk In De Parlor)

MINSTREL SONG

From Albert E. Wier, ed., *Songs of the Sunny South: Plantation and Minstrel Ditties, Negro Spirituals, Stephen Foster's Ballads and Songs* (New York: Appleton and Co., 1929), p. 198.

From the cover of the brochure advertising director Marlon Riggs's award-winning documentary *Ethnic Notions* (1987). Photo from *Ethnic Notions*, courtesy of California Newsreel.

winning documentary *Ethnic Notions* (1987). The film is a poignant account of the various ways in which black Americans have been negatively and derogatorily perceived and treated by white America. The documentary explores the stereotypes of blackness that continue to impact on black-white race relations socially and politically. The film provides an accessible and thorough history of American racism as subtly and overtly presented in popular culture—music, advertisements, household knickknacks, television—and literature. Consider the following examples.

In the 1870s, Bull Durham Smoking Tobacco was used and popularized by Civil War soldiers. The advertisement pictured here is laden with racist stereotypes associated with the black minstrel tradition. Not only is there a connection between black males as animals (horses and bulls) with threatening sexual energy, but the children are depicted as smiling, watermelon-eating pickaninnies. When the visual images of the black characters did not convey their alleged inferiority to whites, their exaggerated, almost unintelligi-

Advertisement for Bull Durham Smoking Tobacco.

ble dialect ("My! It shure am Sweet Tastan") was a clear sign of their intellectual and verbal inferiority.

In the 1940s, a commercial postcard entitled "Black is Beautiful" showed five white men in blackface with two white women. The caption reads, "Overhearing the Kennecott sisters say that they liked men who were tall, dark, and handsome, the guys figured to at least hit one out of three." Such imitations and "playful" use of the image of black men reveal a lack of sensitivity to—or even awareness of—blacks as individuals.

In the 1940s, brother and sister Nidas Dermand (age twelve and a half) and Kathy Dermand (age ten) appeared dressed in blackface as Halloween costumes. Nidas is costumed as Al Jolson, a radio and talking picture entertainer who debuted as a white actor in minstrel blackface in *The Jazz Singer* (1927). Kathy is costumed as Aunt Jemima, a heavy, oversized bosomed black woman, usually wearing a red bandanna on her head and a beaming smile that became a household symbol of black female subservience to whites. Taken in

"Black is Beautiful" postcard: "Overhearing the Kennecott sisters say that they liked men who were tall, dark, and handsome, the guys figured to at least hit one out of three."

Halloween costumes and blackface, 1949: Nidus Dermand as Al Jolson (*The Jazz Singer*) and Kathy Dermand as Aunt Jemima. Reproduced courtesy of Kathy Starbuck.

Algona, Iowa, in 1949, the photographs demonstrate continued racial insensitivity. Clearly, children became part of the white adults' world of black misrepresentation and racial tension. Such deceptively innocent black costumes signaled the larger task of black artists to present blacks without stereotype and caricature.

NOTES

1. Cited in "Archie Bunker, Alive and Well: Stereotypes Die Hard," *Newsweek* (21 January 1991): 59.

2. Marlon Riggs, *Ethnic Notions: Black Images in White Minds* (San Francisco: California Newsreel, 1987), Transcript #1.

3. Sterling B. Brown, "Negro Character as Seen by White Authors," *Journal of Negro Education* 2 (April 1933): 201.

4. Henry Louis Gates Jr., "TV's Black World Turns—But Stays Unreal," in Diana George and John Trimbur, eds., *Reading Culture: Contexts for Critical Reading and Writing* (New York: HarperCollins, 1992), 468.

5. Alain Locke, "The New Negro," in *The New Negro: Voices of the Harlem Renaissance* (New York: Atheneum, 1992), 3–4.

6. Richard Wright, "Between Laughter and Tears," *New Masses* (5 October 1937): n.p.

7. Alain Locke, review of Zora Neale Hurston's *Their Eyes Were Watching God*, in *Opportunity* (1 June 1938). Quoted in Henry Louis Gates Jr. and A. K. Appiah, eds., *Zora Neale Hurston: Critical Perspectives Past and Present* (New York: Amistad, 1993), 18. See other reviews by Lucille Tompkins (*New York Times Book Review*, 26 September 1937), Sterling Brown (*The Nation*, 16 October 1937), Sheila Hibben (*New York Herald Tribune Weekly Book Review*, 26 September 1937), and Otis Ferguson (*New Republic*, 3 October 1937) in Gates and Appiah, *Zora Neale Hurston*, pp. 18–23.

STUDY QUESTIONS

1. What was the Harlem Renaissance, what were its philosophical ideals, and who were its primary writers?

2. Research the roles of music, art, and theater during the Harlem Renaissance.

3. To what extent does racial privilege allow Hurston to present blacks in ways that white authors could not without causing serious social and political repercussions?

4. Discuss the validity of the arguments presented in Richard Wright's critique of Zora Neale Hurston's *Their Eyes Were Watching God*.

5. Discuss the various names African Americans have assumed over the years. Have other groups gone through such name changes? Why or why not? To what extent are the names used to identify African Americans generation-based?

6. Does Hurston present stereotypes in *Their Eyes Were Watching God*? If so, list and discuss them.

TOPICS FOR WRITTEN OR ORAL EXPLORATION: THE NOVEL

1. Discuss the meaning and significance of the title, *Their Eyes Were Watching God*.

2. Discuss the meaning and significance of the two opening paragraphs of the novel.

3. Discuss Hurston's use of biblical imagery in the novel.

4. Discuss Hurston's use of the story-within-a-story structure to frame the novel.

5. Discuss Hurston's use of nature and tree imagery.

6. Discuss the use of humor in the novel.

7. Discuss Hurston's commentary on the institution of marriage as presented in the novel.

8. Discuss the deliberate contradictions in the novel. How do these contradictions contribute to meaning in the novel?

9. Discuss Phoeby's role in the novel. Is her character essential?

10. Discuss the role of Leafy in the novel. Why does Hurston devote so little attention to Leafy's story?

11. Discuss the relationship between Janie and Nanny.

12. To what extent is Nanny a sympathetic character?

13. Identify and discuss the significance of allusions and references to Africa in the novel.

14. What does Hurston intend us to think of Janie's definition of marriage?

15. What does the novel say about mourning rituals in its details about Janie at Jody's death and Janie at Tea Cake's death?

16. At one point in the novel, Janie credits Tea Cake for having "taught me de maiden language all over." Locate within the novel metaphors that define this novel as a consciously "feminine" one.

17. Discuss the role of women's sexuality in the novel.

18. Why does Hurston allow a more eloquent narrator to tell Janie's story at many times in the novel? Is Janie too uneducated to articulate her own story?

19. What does the novel say about education and literacy?

20. What does the novel say about class consciousness?

21. How does Hurston distinguish black culture from southern culture?

22. Discuss Hurston's use of fantastical—the language and images of fairytales—or romantic language in the novel. Such examples include references to golden dust, kingdoms, princes, and magic.

23. To what extent is Nanny a feminist, one who believes in women's right to make decisions about their own lives?

24. Why does Hurston use such literary devices as similes and metaphors to tell the story of "uneducated" people?

25. Is race secondary to the feminist focus of the novel?

26. To what extent is Hurston's novel a "womanist" text, a text focusing on a black feminist whose battle is not just against sexism but against larger social prescriptions for female behavior?

27. Discuss Hurston's use of theater motifs in the novel.

28. In her use of black vernacular—black 'street talk' that is mistakenly thought of as slang—how does Hurston manage to create a reality quite apart from that of the blackface minstrel tradition?

29. Discuss the significance of ritual(s) in the novel.

30. Discuss the role of music in the novel.

31. Read and discuss Hurston's short story "Sweat" (1926) for parallels with *Their Eyes Were Watching God*, especially in terms of Hurston's commentary on marriage and violence within domestic relationships.

32. Read and discuss Hurston's short play "Color Struck: A Play in Four Scenes" (1925) for parallels with *Their Eyes Were Watching God*, especially in terms of Hurston's presentation of color discrimination among African Americans.

33. What is "the blues"? To what extent do various characters "sing the blues"? To what extent is the entire novel or Janie's story a blues song? What is the connection between blues and Negro spirituals?

TOPICS FOR WRITTEN OR ORAL EXPLORATION: ORALITY

1. Define eighteenth- and nineteenth-century American minstrelsy.

2. What is a minstrel show?

3. What is a minstrel song?

4. Discuss the differences between minstrel songs and spirituals.

5. Analyze the language of a minstrel song. What is the song about? Does the song tell a story?

6. View Al Jolson's *The Jazz Singer* (1927) for an example of blackface minstrelsy in film.

7. How do minstrels present African American behavior?

8. How do minstrels present African American speech?

9. What words occur most often in minstrel songs?

10. Do the minstrel songs present stereotypes of African Americans?

11. What do minstrel songs reveal about their creators?

12. Why did African Americans participate in the minstrel tradition?

13. View and discuss the documentary *Ethnic Notions: Black Images in White Minds* (California Newsreel, 1987).

14. Compare the language of a minstrel song and the language in an Uncle Remus tale.

15. Compare the language of minstrel songs and the language of Negro spirituals.

16. Find a recording of minstrel songs. Discuss the significance of the language combined with the music.

17. Research the popular southern tune "Dixie," by Dan Emmett. What is the song about? What is the language of the song trying to convey?

18. Create a folktale that explains something: for example: why the sky is blue; why dogs bark; why beaches are sandy. Be sure to incorporate the narrative and rhetorical strategies of storytelling: dialogue, time punctuations, personifications, performance rhythms.

19. Have an older person tell you a folktale, and record it as it is told to re-create the rhythm of its telling.

20. Make a glossary of words that you think African Americans created and use that have special meanings. To what extent have these words moved into mainstream white America in usage?

21. Make a glossary of words and their meanings that only you and your family know.

22. Make a glossary of words and their meanings that only you and your closest circle of friends know.

BIBLIOGRAPHY

"Archie Bunker, Alive and Well: Stereotypes Die Hard." *Newsweek* (21 January 1991): 59.

Auset, Msingi. "The Soap Spill: African-Americans on Daytime." *Upscale* (September/October 1994): 56–59.

Bassett, John E. "Introduction." In *Harlem in Review: Critical Reactions to Black American Writers, 1917–1939*. Selinsgrove, PA: Susquehanna University Press, 1992, pp. 17–36.

Bates, Marston. "Black, White and Colored." In H. Wendell Smith, ed., *Elements of the Essay: A Reader for College Writers*. Belmont, CA: Wadsworth Publishing, 1981, pp. 449–454.

"Broad Coalition Seeks 'African American' Name." *Jet* (16 January 1989): 53.

Brown, Sterling E. "Negro Character as Seen by White Authors." *Journal of Negro Education* 2 (April 1933): 179–203.

Brundage, W. Fitzhugh. *Lynching in the New South: Georgia and Virginia, 1880–1930*. Urbana: University of Illinois Press, 1993.

Cooper, Priscilla Hancock. *Migrations: A Family's Story, a People's History*. Birmingham, AL: Nia Institute, 1994.

————. "The Oral Tradition and the Harlem Renaissance: An Exploration of Afro-American Literature." Teacher's Guide for an Audio-Cassette Curriculum Supplement. Birmingham: Alabama Humanities Foundation, 1987.

Duffy, Mike. "Leaving behind the 'Aunt Jemima Syndrome': Black Shows Steer away from Stereotyped Image." *Birmingham News* (8 April 1994): F20–F21.

Edwards, Amber. "Against the Odds: The Artists of the Harlem Renaissance." Alexandria, VA: Adult Learning Satellite Service, 1994. Audio cassette.

Ellis, Trey. "Remember My Name." *Village Voice* (13 June 1989): 38.

Emanuel, James A., and Theodore L. Gross, eds. "Introduction." In *Dark Symphony: Negro Literature in America*. New York: Free Press, 1968, pp. 62–68.

"Focus—What's in a Name?" *MacNeil/Lehrer Newshour* (22 March 1989). New York: WNET, 1989. Transcript of show #3393, pp. 1–14.

Gates, Henry Louis, Jr. "TV's Black World Turns—But Stays Unreal." In Diana George and John Trimbur, eds., *Reading Culture: Contexts for Critical Reading and Writing*. New York: HarperCollins, 1992, pp. 463–471.

Gilman, Sander L. "Introduction: What Are Stereotypes and Why Use Texts to Study Them?" In *Difference and Pathology: Stereotypes of Sexuality, Race, and Madness*. Ithaca: Cornell University Press, 1985, pp. 15–35.

Greenberg, Bradley S., and Jeffrey E. Brand. "Minorities and the Mass Media: 1970s to 1990s." In Jennings Bryant and Dolf Zillman, eds., *Media Effects: Advances in Theory and Research*. Hillsdale, NJ: Lawrence Erlbaum Associates, 1994, pp. 273–314.

Gunther, Marc. "Blacks Can't Get a Foothold in Family Dramas." *Birmingham News/PUNCH* (10 March 1995): F21.

"Harlem Renaissance." *Black America: The Sounds of History*. New York: AVI Associates, n.d. Audio cassette.

"Harlem Voices." Birmingham Broadway Series. Humanities Outreach in Tennessee. Nashville: Tennessee Performing Arts Center, 1994. Study Guide.

Huggins, Nathan Irvin. *Harlem Renaissance*. New York: Oxford University Press, 1971.

Johnson, Steve. "Racial Diversity Creeps Back into Fall Prime-Time Line-ups." *Arizona Republic* (16 September 1997): C6.

Lincoln, C. Eric. "Northern Migration." In *The Negro Pilgrimage in America*. New York: Bantam Books, 1967, pp. 84–99.

Locke, Alain, ed. *The New Negro: Voices of the Harlem Renaissance*. New York: Atheneum, 1992.

Lyles, Barbara. "What to Call People of Color." *Newsweek* (February 1989): 8–9.

Miller, Stanley. "Survey: Racial Stereotypes Strong Despite Fight against Discrimination." *Birmingham News* (8 January 1991): A4.

Nelson, Dale. " 'African-American' Not Catching on among Most Blacks." *Birmingham News* (28 January 1991): A1, A8.

Nunn, Ray, executive producer. "Black in White America" (29 August 1989). New York: American Broadcasting Companies, 1989. Transcript #ABC-6.

Perkins, Kathy A., ed. *Black Female Playwrights: An Anthology of Plays before 1950*. Bloomington: Indiana University Press, 1989.

Perlmutter, Phillip. "Who Isn't a 'Hyphenated' American?" *Christian Science Monitor* (31 January 1989): 19.

Pinsker, Beth. "With Better Roles, Black Actresses Can Exhale." *Arizona Republic* (10 October 1997): D3.

"Renaissance and Radicalism, 1915–1945." In Richard Barksdale and Keneth Kinnamon, eds., *Black Writers of America: A Comprehensive Anthology*. New York: Macmillan, 1972, pp. 467–479.

Riggs, Marlon, director. *Color Adjustment*. San Francisco: Resolution Incorporated/California Newsreel, 1991. Video cassette.

Riggs, Marlon. *Ethnic Notions: Black People in White Minds*. San Francisco: California Newsreel, 1987. Audio cassette.

"Should We Call Ourselves African Americans?" In Richard C. Monk, ed., *Taking Sides: Clashing Views on Controversial Issues in Race and Ethnicity*. Guilford, CT: Dashkin Publishing, 1994, pp. 84–100.

Smith, Tom W. *Ethnic Images*. Chicago: National Opinion Research Center, University of Chicago, December 1990. GSS Topical Report #19.

Thornton, Jeannye, and David Whitman with Dorian Friedman. "Whites' Myths about Blacks: Though Some White Views Have Softened, Mistaken Beliefs Persist." *U.S. News and World Report* (9 November 1992): 41, 43–44.

Wall, Cheryl A. "The Harlem Renaissance." In *African American Literature: Voices in a Tradition*. Orlando, FL: Holt, Rinehart and Winston, 1992, pp. 266–278.

Waters, Harry F., with Janet Huck. "TV's New Racial Hue." *Newsweek* (25 January 1988): 52–53.

Wright, Richard. "Between Laughter and Tears." *New Masses* (5 October 1937): n.p. Reprinted in Henry Louis Gates Jr. and A. K. Appiah, eds., *Zora Neale Hurston: Critical Perspectives Past and Present*. New York: Amistad, 1993, pp. 16–17.

2

"Lords of Sounds and Lesser Things": The Role of Language

African Americans are often criticized by white society because of their alleged inability to master standard English. The minstrel tradition of the 1800s found white people with grease painted or burnt cork smeared black faces entertaining white audiences not only through nonsensical language and ridiculous behavior but, most important, through their mockery of blacks' supposed inability to communicate effectively and to articulate clearly. The vernacular tradition, or spoken English by Africans made slaves in America, became for white slaveowners a way of further defining the blacks' prescribed places as inferiors—unintelligent, unintelligible, and linguistically unsophisticated. Never mind the fact that slaves like Frederick Douglass in his *Narrative of the Life of Frederick Douglass, Written by Himself* (1859) defined enslavement not solely as physical bondage but as a denial of literacy, the ability to read and write. A demonstration of the power of words and of word mastery, Douglass's *Narrative* is an exercise in word manipulation and self-fashioning through language. With clever turns of phrases and imitations of classical literary forms ranging from apostrophes to personifications, Douglass makes words bend to his will. As Douglass moves toward literal freedom from slavehood, he moves also toward humanness and self-definition through the vehicle of language and speech.

Even the young slave Phillis Wheatley in 1772 was denied authorship of her own poems because she was believed incapable of such linguistic mastery. Wheatley's test (in Boston, MA) before a jury of prominent white men—among them the statesman John Hancock—centered around language, around what a slave was capable of uttering and writing. When the test was completed, it was agreed that Wheatley had in fact authored the poems in her 1773 publication:

> We, whose names are underwritten, do assure the World, that the Poems specified in the following pages, were (as we verily believe) written by Phillis, a young Negro Girl, who was, but a few Years since, brought, an uncultivated Barbarian, from Africa, and has ever since been, and now is, under the Disadvantage of serving as a slave in a Family in this Town. She has been examined by some of the best Judges, and is thought qualified to write them. (Preface to the First Edition of Phillis Wheatley's *Poems on Various Subjects: Religious and Moral*, 1773)

Wheatley's volume now has the distinction of being the first volume of poetry published by a person of African descent.

Recent debates on Ebonics—the spoken and written black vernacular—continue this focus on the language of African Americans. While African American linguists have for over twenty years documented the rules that govern the speech patterns of many blacks, critics—black and white—deny the legitimacy of such a linguistic reality. Even though the debate is not fundamentally along racial lines, class—the uneducated versus the educated—is at the forefront of those opposing and supporting the acknowledgment of black vernacular as a language and not simply a dialect. What the various debates on blacks' use of language reiterate and accentuate is that language defines identity and that identity is expressed through the language one uses, both written and spoken.

A celebration of black woman's self-empowerment, Zora Neale Hurston's *Their Eyes Were Watching God*, against a backdrop of American racism and classism, foregrounds porch-sitting as a self-fashioning ritual for African Americans' individual and collective identities. Early in the novel, Hurston establishes the porch as a stage where individuals perform and evaluate performance consciously and unconsciously:

The sun was gone. . . . It was time for sitting on porches beside the road. It was the time to hear things and talk. These sitters had been tongueless, earless, eyeless conveniences all day long. . . . But now, the sun and the bossman were gone, so the skins felt powerful and human. They became lords of sounds and lesser things. They passed nations through their mouths. They sat in judgment. (*TEWWG* 9–10)

Fundamentally a tale of people talking—being denied voice and creating voice—Hurston's novel exalts an African tradition of storytelling over what Harlem Renaissance writer Jean Toomer calls "being hypnotized by literacy," a western ideal. As rural black southerners stake a territorial claim in a struggle against western cultural aggressions, they celebrate themselves and their humanness. Giving voice to blacks generally and to black women specifically, Hurston, through the rhythms, cadences, and rituals of talking, explores gender differences in why and how men and women talk and what they talk about. As the menfolk flex their muscles through verbal sparring—as in "playing the dozens," or oral gymnastics—as in the seemingly nonsensical discussion of nature and caution, and storytelling—as in the elaborate embellishments on the mule—the women weave fictions that clothe their curiosities through gossip and imagination. Removed from their immediate economic, social, and political limitations, the porch-sitters are temporarily empowered through oral communion and entertainment. Especially does Janie, Hurston's central character, define her existence and fashion her self through her ultimate participation in traditionally patriarchal storytelling rituals. Crossing socially prescribed gender boundaries that would keep women inside the home and men outside to explore the world, Janie validates herself by telling her story in her own voice. One might argue that the novel climaxes at its beginning, when at the end of the first chapter the narrator states quite simply but importantly that Janie spoke.

Hurston's use of the porch as a setting also establishes the immediacy of theater and drama—a symbiosis between audience and performer—particularly in African American culture. Through porch-sitting, Hurston reveals the rich textures and nuances of black folks talking about nothing and making something of that nothing. Although they seem to talk about nothing, in fact their talking is the something that Hurston aesthetically raises to high art. Hence, for Hurston's characters and for African Americans generally, the porch and the porch-sitting talking rituals become a life source to those denied livelihood and legitimacy in other American social, political, and historical arenas.

An exploration of Hurston's use of orality and rituals of talking to define and celebrate African American culture would address some of the following questions:

> To what extent is African American culture mirrored in Hurston's porch-sitting?
>
> How do the talking rituals of Hurston's porch-sitters differ along gender lines?
>
> What is the importance of voice and talking to those who have been systematically, historically, politically, and socially denied their own voice?
>
> How is the act of speaking empowering?
>
> How does an audience influence a performer's talking?
>
> What constitutes good storytelling?
>
> To what extent are gestures, movement, voice, and intonation— elements of drama—common to effective storytelling?
>
> How does Hurston elevate black vernacular to "high art"—the alleged best that a culture has to offer?
>
> How does Hurston's use of black vernacular and dialect move away from the nineteenth-century minstrel tradition that mocked as entertainment for whites the way black people allegedly talk?
>
> How does Hurston re-create the rhythms and cadences of black people talking?
>
> What particular skills are necessary for Hurston to write a text that sounds familiar to the reader's ear?
>
> How does Hurston write sounds and rhythm into her novel?
>
> How does Hurston effectively present the theatricality of traditional southern black church services?
>
> What aspects of Hurston's phrasings can be connected with the contemporary rap tradition?

The need to talk, to tell stories, is fundamental to human existence; in fact, it separates humans from animals. Toni Morrison's character Paul D in *Beloved* (1987) is forced to wear a bit that prevents him from talking. Morrison details the horrors of this state:

> the iron bit was in his mouth. . . . He wants to tell me . . . he wants me to ask him about what it was like for him—about how offended the tongue is, held down by iron, how the need to spit is so deep you cry for it. She already knew about it, had seen it time after time in the place before Sweet Home. Men, boys, little girls, women. The wildness that shot up into the eye the moment the lips were yanked back. Days after it was taken out, goose fat was rubbed on the corners of the mouth but nothing to soothe the tongue or take the wildness out of the eye. (71)

To legitimize human experiences and to communicate the imaginative workings of the human mind, Hurston launches her social protest against racism, sexism, and classism through language. Through *Their Eyes Were Watching God*, she removes the metaphorical bits—slavery and Jim Crow—that silenced slaves and freed black men and women for over four hundred years. Jim Crow laws were written and unwritten rules in place by World War I up until the Civil Rights movement to maintain black and white social segregation, especially in the South. Such rules as "For Colored Only" or "For Whites Only" separated cemeteries, swimming holes, hospitals, and water fountains. Others involved whites maintaining a superior position by dictating the boundaries of public behavior.

GOSSIP AS STORYTELLING

In her popular bluesy hit "Something to Talk About" (1991) Bonnie Raitt tells about a relationship that others are talking about. Whether or not anything romantic is taking place between the two talked-about subjects—a man and a woman—is less important than the fact that people are talking about this couple and drawing their own conclusions or creating their stories. Raitt's song is an example of the power and allure of gossip. It is also an example of gossip as pure storytelling.

For the most part, gossip has traditionally and stereotypically been associated with the idle chit-chat of women who have nothing better to do with their time and energy than attend to other folks' business. One source claims that distracting gossipers from their own life circumstances, however temporary, spoke to the power of gossip. For instance, women attending to other women allegedly gossiped to distract a laboring mother from the physical pain and discomfort of childbirth. And the juicier the gossip, the more distracted the person listening or participating in this talking ritual became. Whereas rumor is more passive in its transmission with little improvisation, gossip is fundamentally creative and improvisational.

Gossip is a primary talking ritual in *Their Eyes Were Watching God*. From the moment Janie Crawford returns from burying Tea Cake, the question of what her life has been like since she left Eatonville with a younger man has been burning in the thirsty-for-knowledge porch-sitters. Instead of asking Janie directly about her life, the porch-sitters bask in the opportunity to create their own versions of what Janie's life in their absence has been like. If they do not know truth, they create it and pass it around for others to share. Hence, gossip establishes community around the sharing of information. As a talking ritual requiring at least two talking parties about a third, gossip also has a performer-audience dynamic that is controlled by certain formulaic variations: "I ain't one to gossip, and you ain't heard this from me"; "This is just between you and me"; "I don't know if this is true, but . . ."; and "I heard it through the grapevine." It is also directly informed by elements of rhythm, improvisation, performance, and creative imagination—the quintessential components of any good storytelling.

Look at instances of gossip in the novel to address the following questions: Who are the gossipers? When do the characters gossip? Is there a gender component associated with gossip? Is there a class connection to gossip? What is considered worth gossiping about? To what extent is there skill involved in gossiping?

TOPICS FOR WRITTEN OR ORAL EXPLORATION: GOSSIP

1. Discuss the origins of the word *gossip* etymologically. Use a dictionary.

2. What is the distinction between gossip and rumor?

3. Play the gossip game: one person starts a sentence and passes it through to several others to see how it changes by the time it reaches the last person at the end of the group. Analyze what happens along the way. Do you hear what was said or what you think was said?

4. Locate popular songs that deal specifically with gossip and rumor.

5. Look for and discuss television and magazine advertisements with gossip and rumor motifs. For example, a Virginia Slims cigarette ad says: "What you call gossip we call fact-finding." The ad has three women sitting and chatting.

6. View videotapes of Benita Betrell from FOX's "In Living Color." Notice how Betrell invites the television audience to become her gossiping partner. Notice also Betrell's rhetorical formula: "I ain't one to gossip and you ain't heard that from me." To what extent does this character create herself and her own realities by talking to herself about other people?

7. Analyze gossip and rumor poems for narrative formulas and rhythms.

8. Locate a segment on gossip from the comedy show "Hee Haw" that begins: "I'm not one to go around spreading rumors. I'm just not the gossiping kind. . . . Just listen close the first time." To what extent is gossip also a way of entertaining and transmitting news?

9. Analyze the following statement as it relates to gossip and its role in the creation of fiction: "It is the responsibility of writers to listen to gossip and pass it on. It is the way all storytellers learn about life" (Grace Paley).

SUGGESTED READINGS ON GOSSIP

Gossip and Rumor in Popular Culture

"Chris Loves Anita, Not Marcia—Maybe." *Birmingham News* (10 November 1995): A2.

Getlin, Josh. "Giuliani's Marriage on Rocks?" *Birmingham News* (12 March 1997): G1.

"Gossip." Houston: AIM Management Group, 1997. National TV spot.

Gossip by Cindy Adams. *Better Homes and Gardens* (May 1998): 141. Fragrance advertisement.

Gossip by Cindy Adams. 1997. Fragrance commercial.

"Gossip." *USExpress* (14 September 1994): 1.

"Gossip." *USExpress* (12 October 1994): 1.

"Gossip." *USExpress* (30 November 1994): 1.

Knight, Gladys. "I Heard It through the Grapevine." *Gladys Knight and the Pips: The Ultimate Collection*. New York: Motown, 1997. 314530826–2.

Luscombe, Belinda. "People: After l'Acquittal, l'Amour?" *Time* (30 October 1995): 107.

———. "Seen & Heard." *Time* (30 October 1995): 107.

Martin, Judith. "Gossiping Is No Virtue, and If It Weren't for Over-crowded Jails . . ." *Birmingham News* (18 August 1996): 3E.

"Mississippi Still Awaits Governor's Explanation." *Birmingham News* (20 December 1996): A10.

Raitt, Bonnie. "Something to Talk About." *Luck of the Draw*. Hollywood: Capitol Records, 1991. C296111.

"Rumors True: Del Webb for Sale." *Arizona Republic* (27 February 1998): A1, A13.

The Soul Children. "Hearsay." *The Soul Children Chronicle*. Berkeley, CA: Stax Records, 1979. SCD–4120–2.

———. "It Ain't Always What You Do (But It's Who You Let See You Do It)." *The Soul Children Chronicle*. Berkeley, CA: Stax Records, 1979. Audio cassette.

Taylor, Johnnie. "Running Out of Lies." *Eargasm*. New York: Columbia Records, 1976. CT33951.

Timex Social Club. "Rumors." *Vicious Rumors*. Written by Marcus Thompson, Michael Marshall, and Alex Hall. 1986. Danya Records 9645. Cited in Wayne Studer, *Rock on the Wild Side: Gay Male Images in Popular Music of the Rock Era*. San Francisco: Leyland, 1994. 240.

"Twenty Years Later, 'Gossip' Comes Full Circle." *Arizona Republic* (28 February 1998): D8.

"Two Men Subpoenaed in Starr Sex Rumor: Tabloid Says Probe Turned Up Nothing." *Arizona Republic* (28 February 1998): A6.

"What you call gossip we call fact-finding." Virginia Slims advertisement. Philip Morris, 1997.

Gossip and Rumor in Literature

Courlander, Harold. "Songs of Complaint, Recrimination, and Gossip." In *The Drum and the Hoe: Life and Lore of the Haitian People*. Berkeley: University of California Press, 1960, pp. 137–147.

Cullen, Countee. "Scandal and Gossip." In *Copper Sun*. New York: Harper and Brothers, 1927, pp. 61–62. Poetry.

Faulkner, William. "Dry September." In *Collected Stories of William Faulkner*. New York: Random House, 1950, pp. 169–183.

"Gossip: The History of a Lie." In Ann Landers. *Arizona Republic* (28 February 1998): D8. Poetry.

Jones, Jymi. "He Said She Said She Said He Said." In Kendricks Levitt, ed., *Afro-American Voices, 1770's–1970's*. New York: Oxford Book Company, 1970, p. 347. Poetry.

Jones, Mona Lake. "Just Between Us." In *The Color of Culture*. Seattle, WA: Impact Communications, 1993, p. 20. Poetry.

Lange, Kelly. *Gossip (a Novel)*. New York: Simon & Schuster, 1998.

Toomer, Jean. *Cane*. New York: Liveright, 1975. See stories "Karintha," "Becky," "Avey," "Carma," "Bona and Paul."

Turner, Patricia A. *I Heard It through the Grapevine: Rumor in African American Culture*. Berkeley: University of California Press, 1993.

ON NAMES AND NAMING

What's in a name? A lot, according to some parents wading through book after book searching for the right name to label their newborn. There are boy names, girl names, androgynous names, regional names—southern names such as Mary Ellen, Bobby Ray, Jim Bob, and Billy Jean. While some families assume traditional names that remain across generations, others rely on biblical names as markings of their own faith. Even class and economic background impact on name selections. When names are official on the birth certificate, families and friends often rename each other with nicknames that in some cases become a new identity for the person apart from the given name.

There are also intellectual and political motives associated with African American artists and activists of the 1960s and 1970s who abandoned their names' symbolic European imperialist meaning and instead embraced an Afrocentric pride and African heritage. Such renaming came with much ceremony and ritual and meaning. For instance, Stokely Carmichael became Kwame Turr, LeRoi Jones became Imamu Amiri Baraka, and Paulette Williams became Ntozake Shange. This self-selection or tribal naming reflected a significant sense of spirituality and community.

Another aspect of the naming ritual among African Americans is inventive spellings, believed to be associated with African names, such as Shaniqua, Shanta (pronounced Shun-té), and Markisha. Kelly Starling, in her essay "The New Game: Modern Parents Find That Naming Babies Is Not Child's Play" (*Ebony*, June 1998, 116, 118, 120), states, "African-American names today are arguably the most diverse ever. A glimpse at a Chicago kindergarten roster reveals *nouveau* creations like Shaquille, Nefertiti and Zalika" (116). Whether or not the names have any African meaning, their sounds connect them with what is perceived and considered an African past. Through inventive spellings, African Americans empowered themselves and hoped to pass along a strong sense of cultural identity—much like there are Jewish names and naming rituals,

Italian names and naming rituals, Greek names and naming rituals, among other groups.

Throughout *Their Eyes Were Watching God*, Zora Neale Hurston sprinkles character names that break with the tradition of identifying people and being identified by formal "christened" or birth certificate names. Hurston includes the subtlety of naming rituals among African Americans to further contextualize variations on talking rituals and to demonstrate the power and excitement of self-definition individually and communally. Rather than assign names like Susan, Jane, John, Sara, or Rick to her characters, Hurston adds cultural texture to the novel with characters named Bootsie, Teadi, Big 'oman, Tea Cake, Alphabet, Motor Boat, Muck-Boy, Stew Beef, Coodemay, Bootyny, Sop-de-Bottom, Double-Ugly, Who Flung, and LilBit. Notice that the names in these cases may be based on personality or physical traits, particular experiences, or arbitrary choices. What is important in the naming and renaming is that the names are accepted by others, and the recognition of these names signifies another dimension of established community.

TOPICS FOR WRITTEN OR ORAL EXPLORATION: NAMING

1. Discuss the significance of nicknames.
2. How many people do you suppose have nicknames that are included on their birth certificates?
3. Discuss the renaming of sorority and fraternity members.
4. Discuss the significance of rappers' names.
5. Discuss the significance of single names of celebrities: Cher, Madonna, Prince.
6. Discuss Prince's self-renamings and his final one as a symbol, even the "artist formerly known as Prince."
7. What do names say about individuals?
8. What do names say about cultures?

"THEM FOLKS AIN'T TALKIN' RIGHT": GLANCING AT THE EBONICS DEBATE

Between the exaggerated and nonsensical language of minstrel songs and shows and the language of Zora Neale Hurston's characters in *Their Eyes Were Watching God* is a national debate over the language of black folks. The debate began in the 1970s and resurfaced dynamically in the mid-1990s when the Oakland Public School System in California introduced an initiative to legitimize black vernacular as a necessary teaching strategy for African American children being victimized by the American education system. Relegated to slang and deemed the language of illiterates—and therefore worthless by mainstream educated Americans, both black and white—linguists of African American speech continue to argue that the vernacular language of African Americans is anything but random, syntactically unsophisticated, and indicative of blacks' alleged intellectual inferiority to whites, who set the standards for "proper" and "correct" speech. Zora Neale Hurston's decision to record the language of black folk without apology and annotation connects language with cultural identity, value, and self-empowerment.

A glance at the following newspaper headlines and journal article titles shows how the language of black people strikes at the very heart of the illusion of American cultural sameness:

" 'They Done Taken My Blues and Gone': Black Talk Crosses Over" (Geneva Smitherman)

" 'It Bees Dat Way Sometime': Sounds and Structure of Present-Day Black English" (Geneva Smitherman)

"The Elements of Style: Black English Is a Language System—and Here Are the Rules" (Angela Ards)

"We Be or Not We Be: Educators and Scholars Discuss the Miseducation of Black Youth"

"Schoolyard Sages: New York City School Kids Weigh In on Ebonics" (Gary Dauphin)

"Hooked on Ebonics" (John Leland and Nadine Joseph)

"Black Speech Is Talk of Town: Ebonics Debate Rules Convention" (Janita Poe)

"Oakland Officials Haven't Found Magic in Ebonics" (William Raspberry)

"Youz Goin' ta Oakland" (Mike Peters cartoon)

"No Easy Way Out: Alabama School Officials Understand Ebonics Is No Shortcut to Fixing Education Problems" (editorial)

"Straight Talk Missing on Ebonics" (Ellen Goodman)

"Teaching Ebonics Won't Help Students" (Alan F. Clark)

"Oakland Recognizes Black English as Second Language"

"The Color of Language: In Ebonics Debate, All Agree That Race Is Big" (Ellen Hale)

"Not White, Just Right" (Rachel L. Jones)

"Strictly Speaking: Teaching Method No Joke in Oakland" (Nick Chiles)

"Principal Reprimands Volunteer for Questionable Ebonics Assignment"

"What's the 411? Clearing Up the Ebonics Confusion" (Hannah Allam)

"Don't Make Improper English 'a Black Thing' " (Cynthia Tucker)

"Black English: 'Hard to Justify,' Linguist Says" (Robert Rodriguez)

"Black English: Good, Bad, or Just Different?" (Michelle Locke)

"Not All Parents Support Recognition of Ebonics"

"Reverend Jesse Jackson Urges California School District to Reverse Its Decision to Recognize 'Ebonics,' or Black English, as Second Language" (Russ Mitchell)

"Triumph of Black English Gives New Cred [*sic*] to Street Talk: California School's Recognition of 'Ebonics' Stirs Politically Correct Passions" (Arnold Kemp)

"Educators Stick by Ebonics" (Katherine Seligman)

The following essay by linguistics professor Karen Adams defines Ebonics and highlights the continuing controversy that connects the language of black people with deeper issues of identity, intellectual capacity, and social worth.

KAREN L. ADAMS, "EBONICS—LANGUAGE OR DIALECT? THE
DEBATE CONTINUES" (1998)

A language? A dialect? Slang? Bad English? What is Ebonics? Which answer
you get depends on who(m) you ask. For example, when the Oakland
school board declared Ebonics a language in 1996, those who consider
it slang or uneducated speech that is not appropriate for the classroom
were horrified. Some were even surprised by the term Ebonics, combining "ebony" and "phonics," though it had been in use since the 1970s.
Others responded that Ebonics is just a dialect of English whose speakers
are not in need of the same kind of educational help as Spanish or Vi-
etnamese speaking students. So what is the answer to the question from
the viewpoint of a linguist, someone who studies the structure and use
of language as a science? Under what category would we be likely to put
Ebonics?

Let's start with the difference between a language and a dialect. Linguists are always fond of saying that "a language is a dialect with an army
and a navy." We have come to understand that what gets called a "language" or what gets called a "dialect" has nothing much to do with the
actual ways that people talk, but with the status of the speakers who are
doing the talking. As a matter of fact, to a linguist, a language is a kind
of abstraction. Take English, for example. You know that people speak
English in a multitude of ways—e.g., British English, Canadian English,
Singapore English or American English. And for speakers of American
English, there are varieties associated with different regions of the country, with different social groups in these regions, e.g., Valley girl talk, with
speakers from different language backgrounds, e.g., Finglish in the North,
and so on. No one of these is the English language; it is all of these
together, all of its dialects or varieties.

But even as I say this, some of you may be thinking, "Yes, but what
about the Queen's English or proper English? That is really the English
language." After all, these styles of speaking are certainly different from
Ebonics and are declared by teachers and others as "better," and as markers of educated speech. The other forms, such as southern speech, are
often referred to as just dialects.

Again, linguists have a different take on this as they think all people
learn to speak pretty well. We all grow up speaking like those who nur-
ture us. And whatever the variety our nurturers use, according to the
thinking of linguists, this form is "rule-governed." By this we mean that
every dialect has rules for pronunciation, rules for the use of grammatical
forms, rules for the way we order words in a sentence and rules for
making new words. Some rules differ between dialects, but many are

shared. And the rules that teachers discuss in the classroom such as the "who" versus "whom" indicated above are a very small set of rules associated most often with writing and learned by most speakers of English only when they start school.

When groups share a speaking style, it is part of what bonds us into a community. Through this speech we are taught, disciplined and loved. But linguists recognize that as some people move into wider and wider communities, they may find quickly that others do not share this speech and may even criticize them for using it. Children learn at a very young age that some ways of speaking are valued over others. Why do some ways become more valued than others? It has very little to do with the different kinds of rules I mentioned above and most to do with the social power and status of the speakers of a variety. For example, the status of southern speech has more to do with the issues leading to the Civil War, the south's defeat and the weak economy of the south after the Civil War than it does with the fact that southern dialects, including in this case Ebonics, do not pronounce the -r- after vowels in words like "car" or "jar." In other parts of the English speaking world, such as Britain, this pronunciation is considered prestigious because the speakers who say this belong to the highest social class.

Those with the greatest wealth traditionally have had the greatest access to education and have also controlled the media. So their pronunciation and the grammatical forms they use become the language of schools and of literacy. People who do not learn these forms as their mother dialect are capable of learning and do learn rule-governed language, but they may not have had equal access to educational resources and to its speakers.

Why so much controversy over Oakland? Some were horrified for many reasons. First, school has been seen as a place where speakers of varieties that are not "high status" can learn the high status variety and hence enter into communities that expect the use of this form. There is no doubt that school language is a kind of variety of wider communication allowing for shared communication norms among many groups. Some were worried that by having Ebonics in the classroom, the opportunity to learn the "standard" or school variety might disappear. Others were upset because they have always been able to use the school variety to set themselves apart and above others, and the Oakland proposal threatened this status and the thinking that their way of speaking is indeed intellectually superior. For those teachers of bilingual classrooms who have struggled to get funds and help for students from second language backgrounds, the prospect of another community tapping into limited resources was difficult.

The Oakland school board, on the other hand, suggested the change because it meant creating a language environment that recognized the role of the nurturer's language in the community and the rule-governed nature of that language. The language of community teaching and the heritage of the community took on value. After all, Ebonics shares language forms and rules that come from African languages. This is the way that many new varieties of languages come about. Speakers of one language learn another and their first language influences their second. This is one of the reasons why English has so much influence from French. Consider the history of the Norman invasion of England in 1066 A.D. These teachers also may know that even linguists do not agree on whether it is harder or easier to learn a second language or a second variety of a language, but they do know from studies in other countries that using one variety, in this case, Ebonics, to teach another variety, e.g., the standard dialect, could work very well.

So is Ebonics a dialect? Yes, but not in any negative sense that some people might argue. Is it a language? Yes, in that languages are just dialects. Is it slang? As it has informal ways of speaking and formal ways of speaking, it may be used informally as an ingroup way of talking just like Valley girl speech is also often considered slang. But it also has the more formal speech of the pulpit and of community leaders. Is it bad? It is never that, though, now, that depends on what you mean by "bad."

ORALITY AND AFRICAN AMERICAN CULTURE: RAP

RHYTHM, RHYME, AND REASON: THE RAP TRADITION IN *THEIR EYES WERE WATCHING GOD*

There is no shortage of journalistic and media attention to rap and rappers. This attention is usually not a celebration of its form but a questioning of its moral and cultural appropriateness and legitimacy. Just the mention of rap elicits scowls and frowns from many people—black and white, young and old, rich and poor. And much has been made of the profanity, violence, misogyny, and sexual explicitness that for rap phobics have come to define all rap. To conclude solely from selected rap acts and tunes that rap as a musical genre is distasteful, vulgar, and aesthetically devoid of cultural value is to ignore the impact of rap on American culture generally. When the TV character Barney raps about the importance of youngsters having good manners and eating nutritiously, when comedian and actor Bill Cosby raps about Jell-o pudding, and when advertisers use rap to sell everything from bubble gum to hamburgers, it is clear that rap in and of itself is not monolithic, culturally threatening, or aggressive. Rap, as an art form, transcends cultural borders as it is used as an educational and marketing tool.

A primarily male-dominated musical genre, rap as an art form derives from what is generally identified as a "man of words" tradition that emerges directly from African American storytelling rituals and dramatic performance. Such a tradition presents itself in the sermons and speeches of the Reverend Dr. Martin Luther King Jr. and the Reverend Jesse Jackson, and even in the closing remarks by defense lawyer Johnnie Cochran in the O. J. Simpson criminal trial: "If the gloves don't fit, you must acquit." Although it has been used as an effective political tool by social activists, rap is first and foremost storytelling at its most fundamental level. It is also African American poetry, in some instances used to expose and confront social ills. It is African American folk poetry much like blues, spirituals, and gospel. An exhibition of word gymnastics and of talkin' and testifyin' with special emphasis on rhythm, rhyme, and reason, rap is an oral ritual not easily imitated. In African American culture to rap is to create, to improvise, and to luxuriate in the rich textures and nuances of language.

Their Eyes Were Watching God includes many phrases and word combinations that show the richness of folk language in everyday conversations and talking rituals. In fact, not only does Jody Starks "talk in rhymes" to Janie in the early stages of their courtship after she abandons Logan Killicks, but other characters move talking to a level beyond mere talking. They rap.

In this original rap about rap as an oral art form, poet and performer Priscilla Hancock Cooper demonstrates rap as a skillful manipulation of rhyme, rhythm, and repetition. She reiterates that rap as an oral art form has existed ever since people could talk and weave narratives together rhythmically.

PRISCILLA HANCOCK COOPER, "PC'S RAP" (1985)

Some of you think that rap is something new
But I have something to say to you
They say there's nothing new under the sun
And you'll understand when I'm done
That the rap is just an extension
Of this thing we call the oral tradition.

Now I've told you about oral communication,
Call and response, rhythm and syncopation
How these things are passed by word of mouth
And isn't that what beat box is all about?
So you see,
The rap is just an extension
Of this thing we call the oral tradition.

Now I must admit that some of these rap songs,
Have messages that I think are all wrong.
But the use of the beat and the voice,
Just shows that young folks have made the choice
To use the rap that is just an extension
Of this thing we call the oral tradition.

So take this message home with you,
And here is something else that you can do.
Whether in a story, poem, rhyme or song,
You can keep the oral tradition going strong.

Put the rap to some constructive use.
You might even use it to tell the truth.
Because
The rap is just an extension
Of this thing we call the oral tradition.

The following piece compiled by David Donald reiterates the power of rap to transcend contemporary social implications. An exercise designed to teach middle-school students the complicated relationships among gods and goddesses in Greek mythology underscores the power of language and word manipulation that constitutes rap and the African American oral tradition. From the urban streets to the pulpit to the classroom and the courtroom, the influence and importance of rap reaffirm Hurston's notion that the language of her characters from "the other side of the creek" was poetry and high art.

DAVID DONALD, "THE RAP ON MYTHOLOGY: THE GREEKS HAD
A WORD FOR IT—AND IT WASN'T THIS" (1994)

Sorry for the interruption I'm giving no apology.
I'm gonna tell ya 'bout Greek Mythology.
There wuz Zeus, he was the man.
Everyone seemed to be his fan.
Hera was the one he gave his ring.
She wuz jealous of her king.
There wuz Poseidon, king a' da sea.
He could swim much faster than me.
Apollo, Apollo, he ruled the sun.
He could a' burned everyone.
Now that we've told you about gods in Greece,
It's time for us to say, "See ya, peace!"
    —By Ephraim Garner, Chris Todd, and Jesse Wiest

We're gonna do this rap our way.
Learn this stuff and you'll get an "A."
Zeus, Zeus. He was the king.
He sat on his throne and ruled everything.
Hera, Hera, she was his wife.
She was a goddess with eternal life.

Athena was smart; there was no one brighter.
She turned Arachnes into a spider.
  —By Natoniel Scott, Jesse Daniel, and Amanda Oliver

Listen up! Listen up if you wanna hear
About these Greek gods who had no fear.
Hermes took messages from here to there
With wings on his feet he was quicker than air.
Hades ruled the underground.
Beyond the dirt he can be found.
Artemis was the goddess of the moon.
You'll never see her in the afternoon.
We said our rhyme and now we're through.
We hope you study and learn this too.
  —By Quentin Clark, Michael Williams, Charon Taylor, and
  Brandon Scott

Mention Greek mythology and many adults groan with flashbacks of memorizing long lists of strange-sounding names of gods, goddesses and heroes.

Stories about their exploits in a world long forgotten seemed far removed from modern, everyday occurrences.

Simply, the lessons were unconnected and no fun.

"We needed to bring more innovative ideas into the curriculum to help them learn," said Gloria Dukes, a sixth-grade language arts teacher at Myers Middle School.

That is exactly what Dukes has done to a dusty, old subject that has her pupils as excited as—well—as Artemis on the hunt.

By combining Greek mythology with a contemporary art form—rap music . . . Dukes has her pupils seeing how Greek mythology affects our culture today.

And they are having fun while doing what so many people hated to do: memorize names.

Her innovation is not based on the latest theory of how the brain functions nor is it full of educational jargon. Instead, she said it came from her own observation of how she learned to enjoy learning.

"I remembered how I had to learn the states and their capitals in elementary school," Dukes said. "We had to write a song and include them in it. I can still remember them today."

Mythology is an important part of the sixth grade language arts curriculum, and we see signs of the ancient Greeks around us still, she said.

After all, who has not seen a commercial on television, in a magazine or on a billboard for Nike athletic footwear? The name comes from the Greeks' goddess of winged victory.

And reflecting another side of our culture, who remembers that the military chose that name for a missile that was supposed to attack incoming atomic bomb-carrying aircraft in the 1950's?

To get her pupils turned on to the unit on mythology, Dukes had them break into groups of three or four and create their own songs about the gods and goddesses.

Only this time, she used the musical form that a number of the pupils said they listen to and enjoy—rap.

"Students have high interest in the hip-hop culture," Dukes said.

It is their interest that is key to learning, she added.

"If we try to teach things only necessary to be regurgitated on a test, they eventually forget it and it's gone," she said.

The way the pupils can perform their raps or jump into a mythology Jeopardy game at any moment shows how they have absorbed the material.

With caps turned backward on their heads, jackets with leather-looking arms, big sneakers—and a few, white, long-flowing togas—the pupils got up to recite and dance for their fellow classmates.

The performances were good enough so that Dukes videotaped them to show to her other class, giving her students a chance to experience being in front of a camera and critiquing their own work afterward. . . .

The enthusiasm was unmistakable.

"Our group shared what was neat about mythology," Megan Patrick said. "It was a fun experience instead of just talking about it."

Allison Vaughn said working in the group was fun and that creating the rap, although hard, was worth the effort.

"It took three days," she said.

Nicci Boroski added, "You had to relate the gods to real life things."

And without being told, the pupils seemed to have gotten the message about learning, one Zeus and Dick Clark might even understand.

"It was hard at first," Regan Bouchillon said about creating her group's rap. "But it made it a lot easier to learn things. It made it fun so we don't forget things."

She paused, thought for a moment, then added: "It's got a good beat to it."

Savannah Evening Press, 25 January 1994, pp. 9, 12.

SUGGESTED READINGS ON ORALITY AND AFRICAN AMERICAN CULTURE

Abrahams, Roger D., ed. *Afro-American Folktales: Stories from Black Traditions in the World*. New York: Pantheon, 1985.

———. "Playing the Dozens." *Journal of American Folklore* 75 (July–September 1962): 209–219.

African American Pulpit. Valley Forge, PA: Judson Press Editorial Department, 1997.

Baker, Houston A., Jr. *Blues, Ideology, and Afro-American Literature*. Chicago: University of Chicago Press, 1984.

———. *Rap, Black Studies and the Academy*. Chicago: University of Chicago Press, 1993.

Burns, Khephra. "Legacy: Word from the Motherland." *Essence* (August 1991): 44.

Chocolate, Deborah M. Newton. *Talk, Talk: An Ashanti Legend*. Mahwah, NJ: Troll Associates, 1993.

D-Knowledge. "All That and a Bag of Words." *All That and a Bag of Words*. Burbank, CA: Qwest Records, 1995. 945819-2.

Donald, David. "The Rap on Mythology: The Greeks Had a Word for It—and It Wasn't This." *Savannah Evening Press* (25 January 1994): 9, 12.

Dorson, Richard M., ed. *American Negro Folktales*. Greenwich, CT: Fawcett, 1967.

Dundes, Alan, ed. *Mother Wit from the Laughing Barrel: Readings in the Interpretation of Afro-American Folklore*. Jackson: University Press of Mississippi, 1990.

Dyson, Michael. "Rap, Race, and Reality." *Christianity and Crisis* (16 March 1987): 98–100.

Ellis, Catherine. *Tales from Around the World: African Stories and Native North American Stories*. East Sussex, England: Wayland Publishers, 1992.

Faulkner, William J. *The Days when the Animals Talked: Black American Folktales and How They Came to Be*. Chicago: Follett, 1977.

"Fear of a Hip Hop Syllabus." *Rolling Stone* (30 September 1993): 56, 99.

Gossett, Hattie. "Yo Daddy!—An 80s Version of the Dozens." In Carol S. Vance, ed., *Pleasure and Danger: Exploring Female Sexuality*. Boston: Routledge and Kegan Paul, 1984, pp. 413–414.

Gregory, Sophfronia Scott. " 'Diss' Is the Word of the Lord: Profits Being Honorable, Bible Merchants Serve Up Market-Driven Scriptures." *Time* (26 July 1993): 61.

Gross, Linda, and Marian E. Barnes, eds. *Talk That Talk: An Anthology of African-American Storytelling*. New York: Simon & Schuster, 1989.

Hamilton, Charles V. *The Black Preacher in America*. New York: William Morrow, 1972.

Harper, Akiba Sullivan. *Langston Hughes: The Return of Simple*. New York: Hill and Wang, 1994.

Hughes, Langston. *The Best of Simple*. New York: Hill and Wang, 1961.

Hughes, Langston, and Arna Bontemps, eds. *Book of Negro Folklore*. New York: Dodd, Mead, 1958.

Johnson, Angela. *Tell Me a Story, Mama*. New York: Orchard Books, 1989.

Johnson, James Weldon. *God's Trombones: Seven Negro Sermons in Verse*. New York: Penguin, 1990.

Jones, Gayle. *Liberating Voices: Oral Tradition in African American Literature*. New York: Penguin, 1991.

Kwanzaa Folktales. Los Angeles: Time Warner Trade Publishing, 1994. Audio cassette.

Leland, John, and Allison Samuels. "Black Like Who? Rap, Respect and the New Generation Gap." *Newsweek* (17 March 1997): 52–57, 59–60.

Lester, Julius. *Black Folktales*. New York: Grove Weidenfield, 1969.

Levine, Lawrence W. *Black Culture and Black Consciousness: Afro-American Folk Thought from Slavery to Freedom*. New York: Oxford University Press, 1977.

Light, Alan. "Rap." *Rolling Stone* (10–24 December 1992): 79.

Major, Clarence, ed. *Juba to Jive: A Dictionary of African-American Slang*. New York: Penguin, 1994.

McCary, P. K. *Black Bible Chronicles: From Genesis to the Promised Land*. New York: African American Family Press, 1993.

Morrison, Toni. *The Nobel Lecture in Literature, 1993*. New York: Random House, 1994. Audio cassette.

Odum, Howard, and Guy B. Johnson. *The Negro and His Songs*. Hatboro, PA: Folklore Associates, 1964.

Percelay, James, Monteria Ivey, and Stephan Dweck. *Snaps*. New York: William Morrow, 1994.

Percelay, James, Stephan Dweck, and Monteria Ivey. *Double Snaps*. New York: William Morrow, 1995.

Plant, Deborah G. "The Folk Preacher and the Folk Sermon Form." In *Every Tub Must Sit on Its Own Bottom: The Philosophy and Politics of Zora Neale Hurston*. Urbana: University of Illinois Press, 1995, pp. 93–115.

"Rapping Out a Lesson." *Time* (1 May 1989): 59.

Reid, Rob. "Rap Activities for the Library." *School Library Journal* 39 (February 1993): 40.

———. "Rappin' Them into the Library." *School Library Journal* (March 1988): 134.

Ryle, Anne L. "Talk." In Donna Alverman et al., *Little Duck Dance*. Lexington, MA: D. C. Heath, 1989, pp. 118–125.

Short, Gail. "Rapping about Rhymes in Rap." *Birmingham Post-Herald* (26 April 1994): D2.

Sierra, Judy, and Robert Kaminski. *Multicultural Folktales: Stories to Tell Young Children*. Phoenix: Oryx Press, 1991.

Singleton, William C., III. "Yo! Chill and Hear the Almighty Rappin': 'Black Bible' Author Reaching Out to the Streets." *Birmingham News/Birmingham Post-Herald* (13 November 1993): D9.

Small, Michael. "Rap's Bad Rap." *Vogue* (March 1993): 228, 236, 240.

Smith, Arthur L. *Language, Communication and Rhetoric in Black America*. New York: Harper and Row, 1972.

Smith, Bruce. "Gospel in Gullah: St. Luke Written in Tongue of Ex-Slaves." *Birmingham News* (11 November 1994): N3.

Smitherman, Geneva. *Black Talk: Words and Phrases from the Hood to the Amen Corner*. New York: Houghton Mifflin, 1994.

"Talking Brought Me Here: A Nupe Tale." *Springs of African Wisdom: Traditional Sayings of African Peoples (Baya, Ganda, Hausa, Herero, Swahili and Others)*. New York: Herder and Herder, 1970.

Washington, James Melvin, ed. *Conversations with God: Two Centuries of Prayers by African Americans*. New York: HarperPerennial, 1994.

Willett, Henry. "Africatown Grew on Slaves' Legends and Lore." *Mobile Press Register* (1 August 1993), n.p.

ORALITY AND AFRICAN AMERICAN CULTURE: FOLKTALES

Since human beings have been able to speak, we have been telling and hearing stories, mostly short stories. A simple reflection of our daily activities reveals the frequency of the stories we create, tell, hear, and repeat. Such stories not only entertain us and others, but they also contribute much to our sense of individual and collective identity—socially, politically, and culturally.

Folktales are one of the many talking rituals that connect individuals, families, even nations. In *Their Eyes Were Watching God*, Hurston shows the people of Eatonville, Florida, actively creating tales about the mule, tales that involve elaborate schemes of the personified animal. As they further attempt to explain what cannot be so easily explained, folktales create community and are living testimonies of the power of the human spirit and the unlimited expanse of the creative imagination.

The following folktales were written by students in a 1996 undergraduate course I taught on Zora Neale Hurston at The University of Alabama (Tuscaloosa). The students were asked to create an original tale, being conscious not only of what the tale was to answer but also how the tale was being told—words and phrases chosen, rhythm, and rhetoric. In the first tale, Jami Benton offers a variation on the biblical creation myths. Using the dialogue of talking animals, Benton shows the folkloric emphasis on repetition and narrative authority. In the second example of a student's original folktale, Lawana Weaver demonstrates with creative flair the power of dialect and narrative rhythm as her tale explains the stereotype of whites having flat behinds. Recall Tea Cake's mockery of Mrs. Turner who values her Caucasian features: pointed nose, thin lips, and flat buttocks. How does Weaver take a potentially offensive racist stereotype and infuse it with humanity and comedy?

JAMI BENTON, "HOW THE PINEY WOODS CAME TO BE" (1996)

Now I know everyone heard about the way God made up the Garden of Eden and then put the animals and man into it, but that ain't exactly the way it happened. He did make up the Garden, and put the animals and man into it, but the way it was told, there wasn't no trouble at all, that man oversaw the animals and everybody was just fine with it, but that just ain't so. This is how it happened.

In the beginning there was the Garden, and it had some nice little trees in it, but they wasn't nothing much to look at, just fruit trees, about yea high, and some little flowery bushes strewed around on the ground. But that was okay because the animals were just happy to be around and livin'. They had themselves a high time, just sleepin' and eatin' and playin' around. They would talk amongst themselves about how good this God was, to give 'em a playground where they could live in peace amongst themselves. They didn't know that God wasn't through makin' yet.

Well, by and by, God got around to creatin' man and woman, and like the animals, they was fruitful and multiplied. When there was just the two of them, the animals didn't take much heed of 'em; they was just two kinda naked animals that walked on two legs, instead of four. After awhile, they just got to be everywhere, and the animals, they decided they had to do somethin' about all this. Looked like God kinda made a mistake somewhere because these folks was goin' 'round killin' and eatin' the animals that had lived in peace for a long time. So they called together a committee to decide what they was goin' to do about this mess.

"I tell you," said Bro' Bear, "these man-folks is just an all-kinda nuisance. I cain't even go 'round tryin' to find somethin' to eat without them chasin' after me, wantin' to skin my hide right offen me. And you know what they want it for? To wear! Looks like God didn't mix them up just right, leavin' 'em naked and such, that they got to go around tryin' to skin off other folks' fur."

"You right about that," said Mrs. Deer. "They keep a-tryin' to catch me and my babies, wantin' to eat us. My babies ain't got no daddy no more 'cause them man-folks caught him and ate him and then made clothes and shoes outa his skin."

"And what about that damn ole dog, turned traiter on us, helpin' to hunt us down?" said Sis' Possum.

"Well, what we gonna do about this?" said Ole Wise Owl. "God must be off creatin' somewhere else and not takin' no notice of what's goin' on here. I b'lieve we need to get some of us together and go have a talk with God."

"Yeah, that's a fact," said Ole Turkey Gobbler, "but who's gonna go talk with Him?"

Well, they hemmed and they hawed, but nobody wanted to go find God and complain 'cause it just might make Him mad, and nobody wanted to get on the bad side of the Lord. Finally, they decided that one of each of 'em should go. So there they went, a deer, a owl, a turkey, a possum, a bear, and such like. Before long, they realized they didn't know how to get up to Heaven, so they just hollered and called on the Lord for awhile til by and by He come down to see what all the racket was about.

"God," he said, "Here now, what's all this fuss about? Don't you know I got plenty of things to take care of in Heaven without havin' to come down and see 'bout every little racket?"

"Oh yes, sir, Mister God," they said, cause you cain't call Him just plain ole "God" to His face. "Yes sir, we know you got plenty 'a business, but we got a big ole problem right here on Your Earth. Now, we are most thankful for all you done for us, givin' us this big ole Garden to live in, with good things to eat, and sunshine to warm us up, and rain to cool us down, but we got a misery amongst us. You a **good** God, a **kind** God, a **lovin'** God. But it's that man you created; somethin' just went wrong somewhere."

"Are you sayin'," said God, "that I made a mistake somewhere?"

"Oh, no sir, no sirree. We know you don't make no mistakes, 'cause you God. But maybe you just made kinda a oversight somewhere."

And so God said, "I see. This man has been right troublesome to you, has he?"

"Yes, sir. He has been just that. He's runnin' 'round, tryin' to kill us and eat us. Why, he's just nigh about to tear up your Garden, cuttin' such capers."

God just kinda scratched his chin and thought to himself for a minute. Then he said to the animals, "Well, what do you think I oughta do about it. I cain't just kill him off, 'cause I got big plans for him."

"Yessir, we know You got it all figured out somehow, and we wouldn't want to go muddlin' up Your plan. But somebody has just got to go. We ain't talkin' about no killin', just a re-location. We was thinkin', seein' as we was in the Garden first, that you just might give man a new place to live."

God said to 'em, "Well, now, I can't do that. Somebody has got to do the plantin' and reapin'. You all ain't too good at that, so man has just got to stay where he is. I suppose I could just create you up a new Garden."

Now the animals weren't figurin' on this, but they agreed, since it was God they were dealin' with. But they had a few particulars in mind.

"Well, Mister God, that sounds pretty good, but it's gotta be a different kinda Garden. That Garden of Eden just ain't got no where to hide in. Them trees is just too short. Man ain't got no trouble reachin' the top of 'em. He can just pluck some of us right off. And them bushes ain't fit to hide in, neither. We need us a big place and some tall trees and some thick bushes, if it ain't goin' to be too much trouble."

"I reckon I can take care of it," said God. "I'll make up a place, and we'll call it the Piney Woods, with tall trees man cain't reach up in, and bushes he ain't about to stick his hand into. How's that suit you?"

Those animals was fit to bust, they was so happy.

"Much obliged to you, Mister God. We just knew you'd understand our predicament. Them Piney Woods sound just fine."

So God waved his right hand over to the edge of the Garden, and the Piney Woods sprung up from the ground, and all the animals got settled in to their own place, just happy as can be. And that's how the Piney Woods came to be the home of the animals.

LAWANA WEAVER, "WHAT HAPPENED TO THE REST OF WHITE FOLKS' BUTTS?" (1996)

Let me tell you bout the time old Massa challenged John to a race.

Plant my seed in the ground. This is how the thang went down.

Well see it happened that Massa had a slave named John. He was bout seben feet tall and had so many muscles till he looked like a machine— best body God ever put down in creation. John was so big and strong he would have had to ride two mules at once, but the thang is that John never rode no mules cause he could run ever where he went, not even break a sweat, and be back fore his shadow ever moved out its tracks. Now see John could run so fast that he could run by a sign and drag off the words. They put him in a race with a horse one time and John reached the finish line, come back and hit the horse in the behind fore he ever got off the start line.

Well when all the other slaves got to hearing bout how fast John was, everybody started telling John how he could make money running errands for people. They say, "John I bet you could run so many errns that in one week you can git yoself mo money'n Massa." Well, Massa knowed what a fine slave he had in John and it never did bother him that ever body talked about how big and strong and fast he was until they said that John could make mo money. Massa got kind of salty bout that but he tried not to let on, just made like he didn't pay no mind to that nigger gossip.

Anyhow, one day Massa was in town at the dry good store talking to another white man from a plantation in the next county and they seed John pass by the window empty handed, nothin but dust and paper following in behind him. And no sooner than they looked at each other and looked back out the window, John flasht by agin makin 90 and totin enough wood planks to build a house. Then John come back by agin with the letters MR. POE'S MERCHANTILE just advertising they way down the road right in behind him. No sooner than Massa made out what the words say, here come John by agin pulling a cart load of dairy cows wid two pigs tied to each ankle.

The plantation owner looked at ol Massa and told him, "Now that's one workin nigger you got there. He gone have mo money than both us directly."

"Well I aim to put a monkeywrench in his plan yet," Massa said.

Massa flagged ol John down when he come by agin and ast him how much money he'd done made today and John told him and sho nuff he was bout rich as Massa in one day.

"Well John," Massa said, "I bet you all that money that you got that I can outrun you cross the county."

"Now Massa, I ain't one to be bragadocious, but you know you can't outfast me cross this county."

"Well you right," Massa told John, "but I was willing to bet you all my plantation and I'll let all the slaves go free if you beat me. Only thang is you got to cut through the swamp and I gets to usify the road."

John thought on it for a minute and decided it'd be a fair run if n they did it like so. Day of the race they set out. John struck away so fast made Massa's hair curl up. After John done left, Massa hopped on his horse and lit out round the road and threatened anybody that might tell it. Well, John was cuttin through the swamp so fast til the wind caught his nose and opened it up like a two big black sails on a pirating schooner.

Well, John got deep in the swamp and got lost and he thought about how he was gonna lose all his money to Massa, so he figured weren't but one way to keep it. So he called out to a old gator and said, "Mr. Gator you get me out of dis here swamp and I'll give you whatever yo fat belly designing for."

Old gator thought about it for awhile and he said, "Well I done eat plenty frogs, and I done eat plenty scapin' niggras but ah ain't NEVER eat no white man befo. Can you git me one of them?"

John thought on it and said "SHO can."

So gator took John to the edge of the swamp and he run to the other side of the county but Massa was already there so he just ast John for all his money. So John say, "Well, Massa, you know how *theivified* my folks is so I buried my money down in the swamp and you gone have to go git it cause I seed a haint down there when I was runnin through." Well, that satisfied Massa cause he knowed how scary John was. John said "I buried it side that ol gator hole. Just go dere wif your back turned to him and he won't pay you no mind, then you can git the money."

Massa went on down to the gator hole and started walking up to it backwards. Just as he got up there and stooped to look for the money, ol gator bit Massa square dab in the butt and lammed him cross the head wid his tail. Massa hollered out for de Lawd and struck out back to the plantation so fast that he left the rest of that little piece of butt behind. He would have outrun John sho nuff. And thats why to this day white folks ain't got a sign of butt to speak of.

ORALITY AND AFRICAN AMERICAN CULTURE:
SERMONS

When the community mule dies in *Their Eyes Were Watching God*, the townspeople experience a great loss on many levels. The source of much creative entertainment for the townspeople, the mule is talked about and thought of as a citizen of the community. The mule is actually symbolic of Hurston's presentation of the gender roles prescribed to black women—in fact, Nanny advises Janie that black women are the world's mules. Even in its death, the mule commands celebration and introduces a communal spirit common to many a southern black church service. In an elaborate ceremony for the departed yellow mule, the townspeople hold a funeral full of the same drama and performance found on any given Sunday morning when the Spirit is high.

To witness a traditional southern black church service is to witness a very elaborate theatrical performance. In fact, Hurston herself has described such church services as "high drama." With loud vocal responses from members of the congregation and the preacher's gestures, vocal gymnastics, and rhetorical flourishes, such services become art in process, patterns of movement and language always expected but quite unpredictable. Elements of improvisation, dialogue, personification, and rhythm make this kind of performance extremely satisfying spiritually and aesthetically for congregations, who expect and value such performance rituals.

The following are unpublished sermons from two southern black preachers. The sermons offer the same kinds of rhythms as those presented in Hurston's "Sermon on the Mule." The sermons also demonstrate an acute awareness of the power of language to take the congregation on a kind of emotional rollercoaster toward heaven's gate and back. Notice the storytelling rhetoric as well as the preachers' various techniques of dramatization and performance.

In the following sermon, "When I Am Weak, Christ Is Strong," the Reverend J. B. Lester purposefully exhibits a number of performative techniques and rhetorical rhythms. Observe in italics the elements of dramatization, rhyming, and improvisation as well as patterns of parallelism and various phrases and phrasings that punctuate many oral stories.

THE REVEREND J. B. LESTER, PASTOR OF THE PARADISE A.M.E.
CHURCH, JEFFERSON, GEORGIA
SCRIPTURAL TEXT: II CORINTHIANS 12:7, 10
SUBJECT: "WHEN I AM WEAK, CHRIST IS STRONG" (1995)

Let us first begin by saying the words of our text come from Paul, a man who had a spiritual contact with God. When you have a spiritual contact, it not only changes your *heart and mind, but it will change your way of walking and talking. It will change your way of doing, your way of going.* This is what happened to Paul as he traveled from Jerusalem to Damascus, when he saw that bright light that shines from heaven. Not only did it change his mind and heart, but it changed his name. For when he started, he was Saul. But when he got there, he was Paul. That helps me to understand what mother meant when she sang the song, "I Got a New Name in Glory, and It's Mine, Mine, Mine." *You remember how* the Lord spoke to him. *Can't you hear him* saying, "Saul, why are you persecuting me?" Saul said, "Who are you, Lord?" And the Lord said, "I am Jesus." Saul said, "Lord, what do you want me to do?" So he got up from the ground. *His eyes were opened but he saw no one.* And they led him by the hand and brought him to Damascus. And he was there three days without sight. And he neither ate nor drank.

Now there was a certain disciple at Damascus named Ananias. The Lord said to him, "Go down on the street called Straight Street. Go to the house of Judas for one called Saul of Tarsus for behold he is praying." I'm not afraid of a praying man. "For in a vision he has seen a man named Ananias coming and putting his hand on him so that he might receive his sight." Ananias answered the Lord: "I have heard from many about this man. How much harm has he done to your saints in Jerusalem? And I hear he has authority from the chief priest to bind all who call on your name." But the Lord said to him, "Go forth. He is a chosen vessel of mine to bear my name before Gentiles, kings, and the Children of Israel. For I will show him how many things he must suffer for my namesake."

And Ananias went his way and entered into the house. And laying his hands on his brother Saul's said, "Brother Saul, the Lord Jesus, who appeared to you on the road as you came, has sent me here that you might receive your sight and be filled with the Holy Spirit." And there fell from his eyes something like scales and he received his sight and was baptised. And when he had received food, he was strengthened. And then he preached Christ and Him crucified. When they saw him, somebody said, "This is the man who is out to destroy those who called on the name of Jesus. He came here for that purpose so that he might bring them bound to the chief priest." But Paul increased more and more in spirit and strength and he kept telling the Jews who were at Damascus that "This Jesus is Christ, the Lord."

Fourteen years ago, I was taken to heaven. In my vision, I was there for a short time. Whether in my body or just in my spirit, I was there. I don't know for only God can answer that. *All I know is there I was in Paradise. And I heard things so great that they are beyond the power of man to describe or put them into words. That great experience is something to brag about, but I will not brag.*

But I'm going to tell you just how weak I am and how great God is and how God used weakness for his glory. My brother and my sister, it's so good to know that there is somebody who will be there when we are weak. *Sometimes I find myself on my knees* from the burdens of the world. *Sometimes on my knees* with words to say but it's just good to stay there and just mark time. Paul said, "I have plenty to boast about, but I won't be foolish. But I will say this because of the experiences I had were so tremendous. God was afraid I might be puffed up by them so I was given a physical condition which has been a thorn in my flesh. Three different times I begged God to make me well, but he said to me, 'My grace is sufficient for you. My strength is made perfect in your weakness.' "

For I know it is all for Christ's good. So I am happy about the thorn and about the insults and hardships, persecution and difficulties for *when I am weak, then I am strong. The less I have, the more I will depend on Him. Not only will He strengthen me, but He will feed me when I am hungry. He gives me water when I am thirsty. He is my shelter when the storms of life come.*

Finally, my brethren, farewell. *Become complete* but I want you to *be of good comfort. Be of one mind. Live in peace* and the God of love and peace will be with you. *Greet one another with a holy kiss* and the grace of the Lord Jesus Christ and the love of God and the communion of the Holy Spirit be with you all.

My sister and my brother, it's good to know that God will always be there. God will be there when all others are gone. *I hear Him saying,* "If you go, I will go with you. Open your mouth and I will speak for you."

> Have we trials and temptations?
> Is there trouble anywhere?
> We should never be discouraged.
> Take it to the Lord in prayer.

Can we find a friend so faithful—
Who will all our sorrows share?
Jesus knows our every weakness.
Take it to the Lord in prayer.

Are we weak and heavy ladened?
Cumbered with a load of care?
Precious Saviour, still our refuge.
Take it to the Lord in prayer.

Do thy friends despise, forsake us?
Take it to the Lord in prayer.
In his arms he'll take and shield thee.
Thou wilt find a solace there.

I hear somebody saying,

Guide me, O thou Great Jehovah!
Pilgrim through this barren land.
I am weak but thou art mighty,
Hold me with thy powerful hand.

Bread of heaven, feed me till I want no more.
Open now the crystal fountain,
Where the healing water flows,
Let the fire and cloudy pillar
Lead me all my journey through.

Strong Deliverer, be thou still my strength and shield.
Strong Deliverer, be thou still my strength and shield.

Jesus is my strength. *When I get weak, He is strong.* There is nobody
like Jesus.
He is the . . .

Foundation that never shakes,
Truth that never lies,
Friend that never forsakes,
Conqueror that never loses,

Light that never dims,
Beginning that never ends,
Beauty that never fades,
Physician that never "charges,"
Star that never falls,
Rock that never moves,
Strength that never weakens,

Bridge that never collapses,
Judge that never misjudges.

No, there's just nobody like Jesus! And when I am weak, Christ is strong!

The following unpublished sermon is typical of African American church services with all the drama Hurston creates when the mule is funeralized in the swamp. Notice the italicized portions as the preacher's rhetorical strategies: inviting the audience to participate, self-reflection on the process of preaching, repetitions, parallelisms, internal dialogue or dramatization, details of rhyme and rhythm that signal connections with the contemporary rap tradition, storytelling language, personal testimony, and quoting of song lyrics.

"Climbing to Hell" was preached in 1989 at the Shiloh Missionary Baptist Church in Miami, Florida. The Reverend Frank E. Ray is the pastor of New Salem Baptist Church in Memphis, Tennessee. Note in particular how he pulls the congregation into his performance as a versatile storyteller. Notice also his creative flair when retelling and reshaping familiar biblical stories.

SERMON PREACHED BY THE REVEREND FRANK E. RAY AT THE
SHILOH MISSIONARY BAPTIST CHURCH, MIAMI, FLORIDA
(1989)
SCRIPTURAL TEXT: II PETER 3:9
SUBJECT: "CLIMBING TO HELL"

The Book of Peter. Second Peter. The third chapter. The ninth verse. It says, "The Lord is not slack concerning his promise as so many encounter slackness, but is long-suffering to us, not willing that any should perish, but that all should come to repentance." *I'll raise a strange subject tonight.* I want to talk about "Climbing to Hell. Climbing to Hell." So you won't forget the subject, *will you repeat it with me?* "Climbing to Hell." *Allow me to say first of all,* that *Hell is still in business.* We don't like to talk about it, but it's there. We suggest God is such a merciful God that He will not send us to Hell. It is true: God will not send us to Hell. If we go, we go on our own. *Even though God is merciful, He is also just. Even though God is forgiving, He must not change.* So if you go to Hell, you go on your own. *Maybe I need to list a few fellows who are already there to remind you that Hell is in business. As we walk through the hallways of Hell, I hear a brother crying* in the form of a question,

"Am I my brother's keeper?" That answer shouted back is "Yes, you are your brother's keeper!" *I see a husband and wife in hell. It's not good enough for the wife to go, but she took her husband. You're familiar with this woman*: she was the inventor of lipstick, of false eyelashes, of wigs, purple eyes with black face, false fingernails, long dangling earrings. You are familiar with her; her name is Jezebel. *It was not enough for her to go, but she took her henpecked husband to Hell with her.* That's not the only couple there. There's another couple, a husband and wife in Hell. They were trustees of the church. The church was in a building program. It was necessary for people to sell their property and give the money to the apostles. But this couple sold the land, they pulled out their commitment cards, and promised what they made for the guild to the church. Whatever land bought, they had promised the preacher they were going to give it to the Lord. But when they had cashed the check, it was too much to give the church. "It wouldn't bother the preacher, and he wouldn't know anyway. I mean after all he's just a man like anybody else." They came and told Reverend Peter how much they had got off the land. Peter says, "Why is it that you lie to the Holy Ghost?" It disturbed him and when he had finished, he dropped dead. Young men were there and toted him out, and of course he had agreed with his wife, and it's bad to agree to that. I mean if you just stumbled up and you know, lie . . . but when you agree to lie to the church and the Holy Ghost, you are bound for Hell. The wife came in and Peter made her lie. Sometimes we as preachers, we do people that way. We make them lie. The angel says to the wife, "Did you sell the land for so much?" She said, "Yes, sir, I sure did, Reverend, we sure did." He said, "The same men that just took your husband, they on their way back to get you." *They lied and they died.* It's good God is not killing people now for lying. It wouldn't be too many around then. But Hell, *I better tell you*, things happen there that we don't really know about. First of all, *I better tell you*, when you get to Hell, you can see. The Bible says a rich man died and went to Hell and the first thing the Bible says is, "In Hell, he lifted both his eyes." Matter of fact, he could see farther in Hell than he could see while on Earth. On Earth he couldn't see Lazarus on the outside of the gate, but when he went to Hell he could see all the way into the bosom of Abraham. *Lazarus didn't ask for very much; he just wanted the third-class crumb. There are three classes of crumbs, you know. First-class crumbs are the ones that fall from your mouth to the plate. We always get that crumb. The second-class crumb is the one that falls from the plate to the table. If there's no company around, we'll get that. The third-class crumb is the one that falls from the table to the floor.* And that's all Lazarus wanted was the crumb that fell from the rich man's table. He didn't know that *the Bible says, "In Hell, he lifted up his eyes," which meant in Hell you can see.* Secondly, in Hell you can talk because he said, "Father of Abraham, let Lazarus come down, dip his finger on the way in Heaven's water and come down and touch my tongue for I am tormented in this place." *Now,* the rich man had more sense than we give him credit for having because he had enough sense to know if he could talk Abraham into letting Lazarus dip his finger in Heaven's water and that he made it to Hell, one drop of Heaven's water would put out all of Hell's fire. But the Lord told Abraham, "I'm sorry, you had your chance in your lifetime, but now you are tormented and Lazarus is fed." He says, "Now look. If you can't let him come down, I got five brothers I left behind, and when I left they were headed in this same direction. So what you do is go back and *let Lazarus tell them. Let Lazarus tell them.* Maybe they'll believe him. Let Lazarus, a dead man, go back, to tell my brothers that whatever they do, they don't want to come here. Abraham says, "The preacher's already there. *They're doing* their job now. *They're on it, they're telling, they're standing in the gap.* If they don't hear the preacher, the prophet, they will not hear a dead man." *I just thought I'd tell you that Hell is still in business.* "But Preacher, you disturb me when you say that *a person can climb to Hell.* Hell is down. How in the world *can one climb to Hell* when it is down?" *Well,* even though it is down, *the Lord put mountains before us* to keep us from going to Hell. I used to say all the time that it's so easy to go to Hell; but *it's really not easy, it's really not easy* to go to Hell. *When I finish tonight, you'll see it's not real easy to get to Hell.* But *I also tell you,* in spite of it being difficult to go, people are still *climbing into Hell.* First thing *I better tell you* is that the *Lord put mountains before us.* He said, "I am not willing that any should perish, but that all should come to repentance." That way, He wants everybody saved. First mountain He put there is *a mountain called the church, and the church is a mountain.* Whether you believe it or not, the church is not just here for us to have a good time. *The church is a mountain* to keep us out of Hell. *The church is a service station. Not a filling station, but a service station. At a filling station all you do is get a fill-up, but at a service station if your tire is down you get it blowed up, if your car is missing you get it tuned up, if the car is dirty you get it cleaned up, if your tank is empty you get it filled up.* Like so with the church: whatever you need, you can find it at church. You see what's messed up most about the church is we run from it because we say we ain't right for that. *But the church is not designed for anybody to be right. The church is a place full of wrong people getting right. You see the church is a hospital full of sick people getting well. The church is a place full of crooked people getting straight. You see,* if you looking for one where everybody's right, don't join it because when you join you gonna mess it up. That's where *I met the*

Lord. It was at church one Thursday night. *"I came to Jesus just as I was. I was weary, wounded and sad, but I found in him a resting place, and he has made me glad."* If you going to Hell, you got to climb over the Church.

Riding down the street, you see churches *on every corner and between every corner.* If you are going to Hell, you got to bypass the Church. And when you pass the Church, you're going to have to close up your ears because you'll hear somebody singing *"I love the Lord. He heard my cry and pitied every word!"* Let the joy be known! I mean, if you're hungry, don't come to church because you hear somebody singing *"Bread of Heaven, feed me 'til I want no more."* Don't get too close to the church because you'll hear somebody saying, *"Shine on me. Let the light from the lighthouse shine on me."* That is one mountain that you got to climb over—the Church.

But then the Lord give us another mountain that's called the mountain of the Gospel, and *that's what the Gospel do—it's pronounced "God's spell," and if the gospel get in you, it will put a spell on you. Whatever is in you will get a hold on you and come out of you, and people around you will get to know you.* I'm not ashamed of the Gospel for it is the power of God to offer salvation for everyone that believes. But sometimes when people won't come to church and hear the sermon from the preacher, *the Lord says, "Oh, no, that's all right. I will have a saint move next door so if you won't hear a sermon you will see one."* The Lord don't want you to go to Hell. The Lord wants you to go to Heaven. *The Lord say, "Preacher, that's all right, I got the Church, got the Gospel, but then I got a Book."* The old people used to say, *"The Holy Book together is a library within itself." Sixty-six books altogether: Thirty-nine books in the Old Testament, twenty-seven books in the New Testament. In the Old Testament, the five books of the law, twelve books of mystery, five poetical books. Five major prophets. Twelve minor prophets. Four books of gospel. One book of history. One book of prophecy. Seven general epistles. 1,189 chapters. 31,214 verses. 73,486 words. 3,566,488 letters. You got to read it to be wise. You got to believe it to be saved. You soldiers got to practice it to be whole. It's a pilgrim sack, a pie of comfort, a Christian's chariot, a sword. It is universal in its appeal, reasonable in its teaching, reliable in its promise, doable in its content, far-reaching in its vision. This is a mountain. If you're going to Hell, you got to climb over this—if you're going to Hell.* Consequently, *if you just follow two words in this book it will lead you to salvation. I mean if you follow the **if's** and the **must's**. Those two little words will lead you to salvation. Don't the Second Chronicles 7:14 say, "If my people which are called by my name will humble themselves and pray, seek my face, turn from their wicked ways, then will I hear from Heaven, forgive them their sins?" Matthew 16:24 says, "If any man will come*

after Me, let him deny himself, and take up his cross, and follow me."
Romans 10:9 says, *"**If** thou shalt confess with thy mouth the Lord Jesus,
our Shepherd, and shall believe in thine heart that God has raised him
from the dead, thou shalt be saved." John 14:15 says, "**If** you love me
just keep my commandments." John 15:7 says, "**If** you abide in me and
my word abide in you, just ask for what you will and it shall be given."
That's just the **if's**.*

The **must's**—you hear, the must's you will find in *Luke 2:49. Jesus
says, "I **must** be about my father's business." Luke 19:5 says, Jesus enters
Zaccheus' because "I **must** abide at your house." In John 9:4, Jesus says,
"I **must** work the works of Him who sent me when no man ever works."
Hebrews 11:6 say, "Without faith it is impossible to please Him for He
that cometh to God **must** believe that He is, and that He is a rewarder
of those who seek Him. In John 3:7, Jesus said, "I will say unto you, you
must be born again." That's three mountains: the Church is a mountain
that if you're going to Hell you got to climb over. Got to climb over the
Gospel. Got to climb over this Book.*

I'm going to give you another mountain. If you're going to hell you
have to climb over a mountain of Conscience. *Conscience is the best
preacher that I've done ever heard of in all the days of my life.* I've
heard some good preachers. I mean I've heard some that make caps spin
on your head, but when I get tired of listening to them I can turn them
off. You come in on Sunday morning and hear Jack sermon, but when
you get tired, you start reading the bulletin. You'll start punching somebody. Not only do you not want to hear, you stop the lot who do want
to hear. But you can't do *Conscience* that way, no. *When you go home,
Conscience will run riot with you. When you sit down at your table, let
Conscience sit down with you. You may never invite your pastor to
dinner, but Conscience say, "I don't care, I just pray with you anyhow."
You lay down at night, Conscience crawl into bed with you. You say,
"You know, Reverend, I couldn't sleep." Look like witches with you all
night long. Wasn't no witches; Conscience was with you. Some people
can't look you straight in the eye—Conscience working on them. Somebody do you wrong, don't worry about it; you just stay on your knees.
But don't you try to get them. Conscience will work on them.* People
come to me saying, "They talking about me, been lying. I didn't know
nothing about it." Been behind me going, "Oh, Reverend, I'm doing all
right." The Lord want you to be saved, so he placed mountains before
you. *I told you.* It's not easy to go to Hell. The Lord says, "Preacher, you
better tell them!"

Jesus is not in this alone. He has somebody else working with Him.
He used three, there's three, isn't there? The creation story. Father, son,
and the holy ghost. One of those now, is this fifth mountain, you under-

stand me? The Holy Ghost work on you. *When I was a boy* at home bird-hunting, sometimes covered quail would jump up in the air and I would shoot it and he wouldn't always fall when I hit it. Sometimes he would straighten out his wings and float on across the field. I would walk thirty minutes sometimes trying to find. I shot him here, but he floated over there, *the Holy Ghost*. When the gospel get a hold of you, you leave Church and you get the Lord in the cotton field or in an orange grove somewhere. You was trying to mind your own business when *the Holy Ghost* started working on you. *The Holy Ghost*, he do work. *The Holy Ghost, he cares and he shares. The Holy Ghost, he leads and he feeds. The Holy Ghost, he blesses and possesses. Mathematicians can not figure him out. History cannot date his beginning. Geography can't locate his depth. Geometry cannot measure his height. The architect can't paint his ceiling. The electrician cannot improve his light. Uncle Sam can't ration him out. The voters can't stop him. Any of us can't quiet him down. The beast can't eat him up. He's wider than around. He's straighter than a cross. He's purer than air, clearer than a crystal, mightier than a mountain. Tapes can't measure him, water can't drown him, fire can't burn him, Hell can't kill him. The great great Ghost.* No climb to Hell.

We close tonight by telling you the Lord is interested in all of our souls. *Ha!* He claims another mountain just for you and yourself. *Ha!* This mountain add to the other mountains. *Ha! If it had not been for this mountain. Ha!* The church will only be an entertainment center. *Ha! If it had not been for this mountain. Ha!* The preacher will just be an entertainer. *Ha! If it had not been for this mountain. Ha!* The Bible will merely be a storybook. *Ha! If it had not been for this mountain. Ha!* Your *Conscience* would merely be a nightmare. *Ha!* This mountain is called Mount Calvary. *Ha!* No mountain is as important to us as the mountain called Mount Calvary. *Ha!* All the mountains in life are important, but not as important as the mountain that is called Calvary. *Ha! You remember* don't you? *Mount Ararat is where the ark landed when the flood was all over. Ha! Mount Moriah is a mountain where Abraham offered his son Isaac. Ha! Mount Sinai is where Moses went to receive the law from the Lord. Ha!* Mount Carmel is where Elijah challenged the god who answered by fire. *Ha!* Mount Hermon is where Jesus went and was trying to save us. *Ha!* But up on a hill called Mount Calvary, Jesus went there with a ready cross up on his shoulders. He went there, you understand me. *They hung him high and then they stretched him wide. Ha!* The first thing *I heard him say* was "Father, forgive them for they know not what they are doing." It all happened on a hill called Mount Calvary and *I've got a witness here.* I want to stick a pin in it.

If you don't mind, let's leave it just for a moment and let me tell you about a young boy who was good and awkward. He went down to his father's shop one day, sat down, and made a beautiful little sailboat. *I got a witness here*. He painted that boat. He made it with his own hands, went out to the seashore, set the boat out on the sea to see if the boat could float on the water. But to his surprise, a strong wind came by and got behind that boat and scooted it out in the water. He tried to reach it, but it went off farther into the water. He got him a stick and tried to bring it back, but the stick wasn't long enough. He lost his boat way out in the water. He went home crying that evening because he had lost his only boat. Weeks went by. He'd go back every morning looking out on the water to see if he could spot his boat. Couldn't find it nowhere. Months went by. He went out on the seashore trying to find that boat that he made. Finally, he went to town. Walking down the streets, he looked in a souvenir shop and there that boat was sitting in the window. He rushed in the store and said to the owner, "That's my boat in the window." The man said, "I'm sorry, that boat belong to me." And *I've got a witness here now; I heard him say*, "I found that boat out on the seashore." The little boy say, "That's where I lost the boat." The man say, "I'm sorry, but if you get this boat back, you've got to pay what it costs to get it back." *Have I got a witness here?* The boy didn't have any money now. He went on back home. *Started working* in gardens. *Started mowing yards. Picking up leaves. Trying* his best to scrape up enough money to buy his boat back. And finally one day—oh, one day when he got enough money, he went on back downtown, *walked in* the souvenir shop, *emptied out* his pockets, *gave* the man the money, *picked up* the boat, and *walked out* the door. And he began to talk to that little boat, "Oh boat, oh boat, I want you to know you're mine twice. You're mine the first time because I sit down with my own hands and I made you, but you're mine the second time because I bought you." Oh, Mount Calvary, the Lord laid down and died and got up Sunday morning, looked back on a sinful world and said, "You're mine twice. You were mine the first time because I stooped down in the dust of the ground and I made you, but you're mine the second time because I laid down my life that you might get up. Believe in my shadow."

If I don't talk to you no more, Lord, I'm glad! He paid the price for you and your sin, said "You're my children. You have been bought with a cross." I was a lonely island. I was a sinner, too. But I took heart in my master's hand. Oh, Lord! Oh, Lord!

ORALITY AND AFRICAN AMERICAN CULTURE: PRAYERS

One of the many rituals Hurston celebrates is the prayer ritual—not only what is said but also the rhythm and balance of the phrasings and groupings of words. The predictability of the phrasings is what draws in African American listening audiences, who look not for originality and pompous words and terms but for the familiar combinations of words. The prayers also have a clear structure of beginning, middle, and end, and the intonations and rhetorical transitions signal these turns in performance.

The following is a sampling of familiar phrases and phrasings that set church audiences afire during many a Sunday morning worship service.

Father of Abraham, Isaac, and Jacob.

We come before you this morning with bowed heads and humble hearts.

We come before you as an empty pitcher before a full fountain.

We didn't bow here for no shape, form or fashion or for an outside show to this unfriendly world.

We bowed here just to say "thank you" for our lying down last night and for our early rising this morning.

We thank you that our sleeping bed was not our cooling board [the bed upon which the corpse rests and remains cool in a morgue] and that our warm blanket wasn't our covering shroud [any covering used to keep corpse from open viewing, also in morgue].

We thank you for waking us up this morning, closed in our right mind.

Bless the sick and the shut in.

Go into hospitals and cool parching fevers.

Bless those behind prison walls.

Teach us how to pray and what to pray for.

Go with us and stand by us. Protect us.

And when we've gone the last mile of the way. When we've gone into our room to come out no more, we want you to give us a home somewhere in your kingdom where we can praise your name better than we can down here.

This is your humble servant's prayer.

These and other blessings we ask in thy son Jesus's name.

Amen and thank God!

SUGGESTED READINGS ON SERMONS, PRAYERS, AND CHURCH SERVICES

Angelou, Maya. *I Know Why the Caged Bird Sings*. New York: Bantam, 1971, pp. 27–37.

Breuer, Lee. *The Gospel at Colonus*. New York: Theater Communications Group, 1989.

Cooper, Grace. "Black Preaching Style in James Weldon Johnson's *God's Trombones*." *Middle Atlantic Writers Association Review* 4 (1989): 13–16.

Cullen, Countee. "And the Walls Came Tumblin' Down." *Bookman* 66 (1927): 221–222.

Davis, Charles T. "The Heavenly Voice of the Black American." In Joseph P. Strelka, ed., *Anagogic Qualities of Literature*. University Park: Pennsylvania State University Press, 1971, pp. 107–119.

Davis, Gerald. *I Got the Word in Me and I Can Sing It, You Know: A Study of the Performed African-American Sermon*. Philadelphia: University of Pennsylvania Press, 1985.

Davis, Ossie. *Purlie Victorious: A Comedy in Three Acts*. New York: Samuel French, 1989.

Du Bois, W.E.B. "Of Our Spiritual Strivings." In *The Souls of Black Folk*. New York: Penguin, 1982, pp. 43–53.

———. "Of the Faith of the Fathers." In *The Souls of Black Folk*. New York: Penguin, 1982, pp. 210–225.

Hubbard, Dolan. "The Black Preacher Tale as Cultural Biography." *College Language Association Journal* 30 (1987): 328–342.

Hughes, Langston, and Arna Bontemps, ed. "The Amen Corner: Sermons, Prayers, and Testimonials." In *Book of Negro Folklore*. New York: Dodd, Mead, 1958, pp. 225–277.

Hurston, Zora Neale. *Jonah's Gourd Vine*. New York: Harper and Row, 1990, pp. 25, 88–89, 106, 174–182.

———. *The Sanctified Church: The Folklore Writings of Zora Neale Hurston*. Berkeley, CA: Turtle Island Foundation, 1981, pp. 79–107.

Johnson, James Weldon. *God's Trombones: Sermons in Verse*. New York: Penguin, 1990.

————. *God's Trombones: Sermons in Verse*. The Complete Live Production. Saint Paul, MN: Penguin/High Bridge Audio, 1993. Audio cassette.

March, J. M. "Is Negro Exhorting High Art, Too?" *New York Evening Post* (8 August 1927): 9.

"Poetry and Eloquence of the Negro Preacher." *New York Times Book Review* (19 June 1927): 11.

Rosenberg, Bruce. *Can These Bones Live? The Art of the American Folk Preacher*. Urbana: University of Illinois Press, 1988.

Whalum, Wendall Phillips. "James Weldon Johnson's Theories and Performance Practices of Afro-American Folksong." *Phylon* 32 (1971): 383–395.

White, Walter. "Play All over God's Heaven." *World* (19 June 1927): 8.

AFRICAN AMERICANS WHIRLING, TWIRLING, AND CREATING THEMSELVES THROUGH WORDS

When Zora Neale Hurston was a graduate student at Barnard College, her research assignment from the anthropologist Franz Boaz was to go south and collect folklore from the place and people of her Florida origins. While the task might have seemed simple to some—just recording what they heard black people saying—Hurston did more than record the idioms, folktales, and other talking rituals that characterized and defined the people she knew intimately. In *Their Eyes Were Watching God* she documents and celebrates the artfulness of black folks' language by re-creating the energy, rhythm, and textures of words that dance and sing. Hurston's trained ear for language sounds and language sense with many nuances is at the center of her novel about common folk talking and creating themselves through their talking.

As a document of black people talking, the novel presents language with meanings derived not from literal interpretations but from rhythm and communal ritual. Hence, for those unfamiliar with black vernacular culture in the novel, Hurston affords an opportunity for newcomers to learn the culture as they are submersed in it. *Their Eyes Were Watching God* is indeed an unannotated glossary of expressions, words, and sayings that prove blacks' tremendous facilities with figurative language, language gymnastics, and language encoding. Identified by African American scholar Henry Louis Gates Jr. as a "speakerly text," *Their Eyes Were Watching God* is meant to be read aloud and heard. It is a careful articulation of the power of black folks to define themselves through the language they create over and over again. As part of an assignment to get my own students to focus on language codes within African American communities, I asked them to jot down words, phrases, and expressions that they thought had usage primarily among African Americans.

Students should examine the following lists—including phrases and words from Hurston's novel, phrases from Spike Lee's movie *Do the Right Thing* (1989), and phrases from a survey of undergraduate students—to discuss African American language codes.

Even though such linguistic violations are deemed "slang" by a dominant culture that identifies "standard" English as a sign of high culture and intelligence, Hurston moves the "colloquial universal" vernacular language of black folks to the level of high art; it connects a people's identity to the words they create and use, words that have meaning only to those who are familiar with or participate in the culture.

Students should discuss the meanings of words from the lists, noting especially words and expressions that are difficult to translate in "standard" English. They should also discuss the extent to which some of these words have become part of "mainstream" America's language. Students might add words, phrases, and intonations to these lists. They might discuss the implications of these language codes in terms of gender, class, and age. A discussion of the lists should move students toward addressing the following questions: To what extent do the rhythms of words contribute to their meanings? To what extent is language meaning derived from "performing" the language with gestures and other body movements?

GLOSSARY

Ain't

Ain't going to have none of that

Ain't no thang

Ain't no thing

Ain't nuttin' but a thang

All right (as an answer to *hello*)

All that

Alley (behavior that is unsophisticated)

Are you down?

Ax (instead of *ask*)

Ax you a question

Back in the day

Bet'not (better not)

Big pimp

Black as tar, Tar Baby

Blaze up

Bootsee (a wannabe) (a person who wants to and tries to be someone else)

Brang it on!

Bro (friend)

But anyway!

Caintchi dontchi hair (nappy hair you can't comb and don't try to comb)

Can you hang?

Carry me (agree with me)

Case quarter (as in *Can I borrow a case quarter?*)

Child please!

Chillin'

Click (gang)

Collective use of *Sistah* or *Brothah*

Coolin' with my homeys

Cracka (white person)

Cracker

Cuz (because)

Cuz (friend/cousin)

D'as da cornbread; d'as da collard greens (this is good)

Dirt ugly (just plain ugly)

Diss (to insult or disrespect)

Don' even front; quit frontin' (stop pretending)

Don't even go there

Don't go there (shut up)

Don't let me catch you slippin'!

Don't make me read you like the Bible from Genesis to Revelations.

Don't play yourself. (Don't make a mistake.)

Dope (stupid)

Down like fo' flat tires

Down wid it

Down wit

Dy-no-mite!

Estelle does not live here.

Everybody ain't able!

Fat pockets (wealthy)

Feel like a broke-neck dead dog

Finna (as in *Where you finna go?*)

5–0 (police)

Fluids (alcohol)

Fo (for or four)

For real though

Funky

Get to steppin'

Girl

Girlfriend (as in *You go, girlfriend!*)

Girrrrl!

Gitchu sum

Give me skin (slap my hand)

Goin' clubbin' (partying)

Gone do it (going to do it)

Good hair

Got it goin' on

Got some play (as in *Whatchu doing to let me get some play?*)

Gotta meal (eat)

Gul (girl)

Have you got change for a funk?

Have you hit that yet? (sex)

He ain't hurt

He en do it right (He didn't do it correctly)

He got game (good ballplayer)

Here I go

He's a hound (men always looking for women for sex)

He's fat (he's rich)

Hey lil shawty (when speaking to someone; child or short girl)

Hi you gon' act?

High yellow heifer

Holla if ya hear me!

Honey chile

Hoochie Mama

Hood

Hooptie (car)

Hops (leaping ability)

How 'bout

I ain't even gonna go there.

I ain't trying to hear that.

I betcha . . .

I don't feel you.

I got a who-ride. (short for hoop-tie)

I got flavah.

I got game.

I got on some new kicks.

I got to slip back to the crib.

I know you didn't . . .

I reckon

I see you (I understand and agree)

If the Lord is willing

I'll holler at ya!

I'm blowed.

I'm 'bout to get my groove on!

I'm catchin' hell.

I'm down with that.

I'm fixin' to do something.

I'm through wit you.

In the Hood

Is that what it is?

It be's that way sometimes.

It's all good.

It's da bomb.

It's just a thing (doesn't mean much)

It's on (like fight or party)

It's on how!

Jam (dance, music)

Jim Crow

Juice (power)

Just chillin'

Just tryin' to make some ends

Keep it on the down-low

Kick it

Know what I'm sayin'?

Lawd a mercy!

Lawd, lawd, lawd!

Let me tell you something.

Let's get twisted.

Let's kick it; When can we kick it?

Let's make ends; gotta make ends meet (money)

Like butta

Living large (well off)

Ma dear

Mackin'

Mackin' with the homeys

Mad loot

Mane (man)

Mash that (push that)

Me and mine

Mic daddy mac

Mmm Hmm

Mo'

Mo' money

Mutha/Brutha

My ace boon coon

My brotha

Nappy-headed

Naw

Naw Boss

Nice wheels (car)

No mo'

Noren

Nothin' but a thang

Old school (past experience)

On the real

Pack a gat (having a gun in one's possession)

Peace out (goodbye)

Peep dis or peep dat

Piss-po (poorer than poor; bad)

Played out

Player

Popotes (police)

Posse

Pouncil (pencil)

Preach de gospel

Props (respect)

Quit trippin!

Raise up

Read you (as in *Don't let me have to read you in front of all yo homeys!*)

Recognize

Say it one mo' gin'!

Say wudd (say what?)

Scanch

School ya

Settle the score (make all things equal)

Seven-up

She ain't hittin-a-lick at a snake (worthless)

She en (she didn't as in *She en do it right*)

She put her foot in it (the food was good)

She so fly.

She/he gone

She/he is just trying to be white.

Shet yo mouf

Sho nuff (sure enough)

Sho you right!

Shoooot

Shorty-got it goin' on

Shoul is

Sisco

Sistah friend

Skeazer; you'z a skeazer (no good)

Slow ya roll

So black you Blue

Some mo (some more)

Squares (cigarettes)

Squash it!

Step off

Stop da madness!

Stop sweatin' me!

Straight

Straight trippen

'Sup (what's up?)

Swerve on (get my swerve on)

Takin' it back to the alley

Talk to da hand

Talk to the hand

Tell him how many white folks I killed before I found out it's against the law.

That's dope.

That's ma boy dare.

That's straight.

That's the bomb.

That's the cornbread.

That's the lick.

That's tight.

The bear got me.

The blacker the berry, the sweeter the juice.

The chronic

The hood (neighborhood)

The lawd will make a way!

The Man (man in charge; leader; white landlord)

The white man (system) keeps black people down.

There it is.

They were all in my grill.

They were jonin' her! (like joking on her)

Those rims are phat.

Threads (clothes)

Toe up from the flo-up (ugly)

Tore down

Tow-down

Trash (dope)

True dat; true (someone else is correct/making a correct statement)

U-B-trippin'

Um finna eat, go, etc.

Wack (stupid)

Watch yourself now!

We family.

We fin de vamp.

We like that.

Whaddup?! (greeting)

What I'm gonna do withchu?

What up?! (combination of interrogation and exclamation)

Whatchya know good?

What's goin on?

What's that all about?

What's up?

What's up boo? (affectionate nickname for a girl)

What's up cheese? (women)

What's up dog?

What'z up

Whaz up?

Wheels (car)

Where do you stay at now?

Who you talkin' to?

Wide open

W'ontchoo (why don't you?)

Word (you're right)

Word up

Y'all

Yard ($100)

Yo mama!

You a OG?

You bent (wrong, weird, not all there)

You bettah get up off me . . .

You don bumped your head!

You go!

You go, girl!

You gon' be like that?

You got some beef with me?

You know

You know what I'm sayin'

You so crazy!

You straight crazy

You trippin'

You wanna be down

You wrong fo' dat

BLACK FOLKS TALKIN' THAT TALK: WORDS AND PHRASES

(from music, celebrities, movies, cultural patterns—local, regional, generational, gender-specific):

Ace

Ace boon coon

Ain't nothin' but a "thang," or Ain't nothin but a "G" thang (It's not all that important)

Ain't nothin' goin' on but the rent.

Ain't studying you

All I got to do is stay black and die. (You can't make me do anything I don't want to do)

Amen, lights! (signifyin')

Amen, walls! (signifyin')

And that's all she wrote

Bad to the bone

The bigger they are, the harder they fall.

Black is earnest; yellow is so low-down.

The blacker the berry, the sweeter the juice.

Boning (Spike Lee's euphemism for sex)

Bust a cap

Bust a move

Case closed!

Check it out. (not a library phrase)

Check yourself. (Be careful.)

Chill out!

Chitlins

CPT (Colored People's Time; events always starting later than they are scheduled)

Cracking

Crib

Cuttin' up

'Dammit, I'll bite cha' hair (describes another's unruly hair)

Diss (putting someone down by insulting)

Dogging her/him out (giving someone a hard time)

Doing the 'wild thang' (rapper Ton Loc's phrase for sex)

Dude

Eat up with ugly (very ugly)

Everybody say hooooooo! (used during dancing and singing parties)

Flygirl (from "In Living Color" comedy show)

Flyguy

Frontin' (pretending)

Funky

Get down. (Do it well.)

Get on the good foot.

Get outta here!

Get over it. (Stop worrying about it.)

Get with the program. (Pay attention.)

Ghetto booty

Girlfriend . . .

Givin' him/her down the country (being really hard on someone)

Go 'head

Go on, girl.

Go on with yo bad self. (I'm pleased with what I see)

Go Sherry! Go Sherry! Go Sherry! (as chant)

Got you told

Gotta see a man about a mule

Groovin'

Heard it through the grapevine

"Hello" (as signifyin')

Hit it a lick and a promise

Homeboy

Homegirl

Homey

Homey don't play that!

Honey, hush!

Honey, please!

Hurt (ugly)

Hush yo fuss!

Hush yo mouth!

I can read you like a book. (I understand you perfectly.)

I hate it. (I'm sorry.)

I *know* that's right! (I agree.)

I wanna see your tootsie roll.

If I'm lyin', I'm flyin'. (I'm telling the truth.)

If you talked about, you thought about. (People can't or don't talk about you—as in gossip—unless they think about you.)

I'm going to pick a mess of salad.

I'm just a little piece of leather, but I'm well put together. (I'm not as big as you physically, but I can hold my own in any battle with you.)

I'm not down with that. (I disagree.)

I'm scareda you.

In the house

Ink bink, bottle stink

It's a black "thang." (Only blacks can understand.)

Joning

Knocking boots

Later (see you later or goodbye)

Let me put a bug in your ear. (Let me tell you a secret.)

Let the doorknob hit ya where the good Lord split you.

Let's get busy. (Arsenio Hall's phrase)

Let's get it on. (Marvin Gaye's song title)

Licking stick.

Man, please.

Miss Ann (any white woman; southern segregation term)

Miss Thang

Mister Cholly (any white man; southern segregation term)

My name is Wess, and I ain't in this mess. (I'm not getting involved in this matter.)

My "partner"

Nose is *wide* open

Onion (backside)

Pad (place where you live)

Partner

Party over here

Po as a snake (person has no money)

Pot to piss in (poor; as in *He ain't got a pot to piss in*.)

Pump it up.

Pump up the jam.

Right on! Right on to the bone!

Shake yo groove thang.

Shake your money maker.

Sharp as a tack!

Shonough

"Shoop" (Salt-n-Pepa's phrase)

Shut yo mouth.

Skins

Smack the black offa you.

Smack the taste outta yo mouth.

Smokin' (looking good)

Some'teat (something to eat)

Spoke you out

Strut you stuff

Take a chill pill. (Stop getting so upset.)

TCB (Taking Care of Business)

Tell it! (Tell the truth!)

The day you swing your hand at me, you'll draw back a nub!

The "hood"

They look like some of Miss Haggie's chillun. (They are ugly people.)

Tighten up

Too cute. (It was *too* cute.)

Too tough. (He was *too* tough.)

Turn this motha out

Wannabee

We be jammin' (We were/are partying.)

Went off (She caught her man with that thang down the street and she went off.)

Whaddup?

What you see is what you get, and you ain't seen nothin' yet.

What's going down?

What's going on?

What's happening?

What's up?

What's up? Chicken butt. Go 'round the house and lick it up, 5 cents a cup.

What's up, G?

What's your name, Puddin' tane. Ask me again, I'll tell you the same.

White liver

Whoop, there it is!

Ya dig?

Yo baby yo!

You better check yourself. (Be careful.)

You better say it.

You can't lose with the stuff I use. (Rev. Ike's phrase)

You down with OPP? (other people's property; infidelity)

You got it.

You sharp as a tack and rusty as a nail.

You trippin'

Your eyes may shine, your teeth may grit. But none of this you'll ever get.

SPIKE LEE'S LANGUAGE FROM *DO THE RIGHT THING* (1989)

And when your father comes home, he's gonna wear ya little narrow behind out.

are dogged

buggin

dissing

Doctor

doing the nasty

Don't start no shit, won't be no shit.

Fool, you're thirty cents away from a quarter.

House him

iced

is down

is kicking

to be bested

to the curb

Y'all can't even pee straight.

yoke him

you got my back

You're raggedy as a roach.

HURSTON ELEVATING IDIOMS IN THE NOVEL

Lemme know when dat ole pee-de-bed is gone.

They's a lost ball in de high grass.

If dat wuz *mah* wife . . . Ah'd kill her cemetery dead.

Ah'm uh bitch's baby round lady people.

Y'all ain't got enough [land] here to cuss a cat on without gittin' yo' mouf full of hair.

Yo' feet ain't mates.

De ole folks say "de higher de monkey climbs de mo' he show his behind."

Ah'm gointah run did conversation from uh gnat heel to uh lice.

See yah later, tell you straighter.

Ah wuz all over 'im lak gravy over rice. . . . He wuz hollerin' for me tuh turm him loose, but baby, Ah turns him every way *but* loose.

Dat lil eyeful uh bacon for me and all mah chillun!

Ah'll take and beat yo' head flat as uh dime.

Tell me, what post office did *you* pee in?

SUGGESTED READINGS ON WORDS

Daniel, Jack L. "Towards an Ethnography of Afroamerican Proverbial Usage." *Black Lines* 3 (Winter 1972): 3–12.

D-Knowledge. "All That and a Bag of Words." *All That and a Bag of Words*. Burbank, CA: Qwest Records, 9. 1995. 945819-2.

Hardy, Jeff. "Preserving Thousands of Southern Sayings Can Make You as Dizzy as Trout in Blender." *The Mobile Register* (4 July 1993): 3C.

Hughes, Langston, and Arna Bontemps, eds. "Harlem Jive." In *Book of Negro Folklore*. New York: Dodd, Mead, 1958, pp. 477–497.

Hurston, Zora Neale. "Characteristics of Negro Expression." In *The Sanctified Church: The Folklore Writings of Zora Neale Hurston*. Berkeley, CA: Turtle Island Foundation, 1981, pp. 49–55.

———. "Harlem Slanguage." In *Zora Neale Hurston: The Complete Stories*. New York: HarperPerennial, 1995, pp. 227–232.

———. "Story in Harlem Slang: Jelly's Tale." In *Zora Neale Hurston: The Complete Stories*. New York: HarperPerennial, 1995, pp. 127–138.

Levinson, Arlene. "Cracker or Crackerhead: Loaded Words Divisive." *Birmingham News* (25 September 1994): A11.

———. "Language Nearing a Racial Crossroads." *Birmingham News* (25 September 1994): A1, A12.

Smitherman, Geneva. "Appendix A: Some Well-Known Black Proverbs and Sayings." In *Talkin' and Testifyin': The Language of Black America*. Boston: Houghton Mifflin, 1977, pp. 245–246.

———. "Appendix B: Get Down on Black English/Sounds and Structure." In *Talkin' and Testifyin': The Language of Black America*. Boston: Houghton Mifflin, 1977, pp. 247–250.

———. "Appendix C: Black Semantics—A Selected Glossary." In *Talkin' and Testifyin': The Language of Black America*. Boston: Houghton Mifflin, 1977, pp. 251–259.

SELECTED BIBLIOGRAPHY ON AFRICAN AMERICANS AND LANGUAGE

Alexander, C. F. "Black English Dialect and the Classroom Teacher." *Reading Journal* 33 (1980): 304–307.

Allam, Hannah. "What's the 411? Clearing Up Ebonics Confusion." *Oklahoma Daily* (23 January 1997): 1–2.

Aponte, Wayne Lionel. "Say Brother: 'Talkin' White.'" *Essence* (January 1989): 11.

Ards, Angela. "The Elements of Style: Black English Is a Language System—and Here Are the Rules." *Village Voice* (14 January 1997): 36–37.

Armstrong, Robb. "Jump Start." *Birmingham News* (16 March 1997): n.p. Cartoon.

Baldwin, James. "If Black English Isn't a Language, Then Tell Me, What Is?" In *The Price of the Ticket: Collected Nonfiction, 1948–1985.* New York: St. Martin's Press, pp. 649–652.

Chambers, John W., ed. *Black English: Educational Equity and the Law.* Ann Arbor, MI: Karoma, 1983.

Chiles, Nick. "Strictly Speaking: Teaching Method No Joke in Oakland." *Arizona Republic* (14 June 1998): E12–E13.

Clark, Alan F. "Teaching Ebonics Won't Help Students." *Birmingham News* (29 December 1996): C2. Editorial.

"The Controversy over Black English." *Phi Delta Kappan* (February 1980): 101–102.

Davis, Ossie. "The English Language Is My Enemy!" *Negro History Bulletin* 30 (April 1967): 18.

Dillard, J. L. *Black English: Its History and Usage in the United States.* New York: Random House, 1972.

"Education: Outcry over Wuf Tickets: Black English vs. Standard Usage in the Courtroom." *Time* (August 1979): 101–103.

Farb, Peter. "Linguistic Chauvinism." In Janet Madden-Simpson and Sara M. Blacke, eds., *Emerging Voices: A Cross-Cultural Reader.* Philadelphia: Holt, Rinehart and Winston, 1990, pp. 201–208.

Ferguson, Anna Marie. "A Case for Teaching Standard English to Black Students." *English Journal* (March 1982): 38–40.

Goodman, Ellen. "Straight Talk Missing on Ebonics." *Birmingham Post-Herald* (28 December 1996): C2.

Hale, Ellen. "The Color of Language: In Ebonics Debate, All Agree That Race Is Big." *Journal and Courier* (22 January 1997): A1.

Harden, Andrea. "Learn about Ebonics Issue: Ebonics Is Commonly Misunderstood." *Oklahoma Daily* (23 January 1997): 4.

Holton, Sylvia Wallace. "Black English: Linguists and Speakers Today." In *Down Home and Uptown: The Representation of Black Speech in American Fiction.* Rutherford, NJ: Fairleigh Dickinson University Press, 1984, pp. 34–64.

Johnson, Kirk A. "What's IQ Got 2 Do with It?" *Heart & Soul* (August–September 1995): 65–70.

Jones, Rachel L. "My Turn: Not White, Just Right." *Newsweek* (10 February 1997): 12–13.

———. "What's Wrong with Black English." In Janet Madden-Simpson and Sara M. Blake, eds., *Emerging Voices: A Cross-Cultural Reader.* Philadelphia: Holt, Rinehart and Winston, 1990, pp. 208–210.

Jordan, June. "Nobody Mean More to Me Than You and the Future Life of Willie Jordan." In *On Call: Political Essays*. Boston: South End Press, 1985, pp. 123–139.

Labov, William. *Language in the Inner City: Studies in the Black English Vernacular*. Philadelphia: University of Pennsylvania Press, 1972.

Leland, John, and Nadine Joseph. "Hooked on Ebonics." *Newsweek* (13 January 1997): 78–80.

Lewis, Claude. "Too Many Blacks Don't Speak English Correctly." *Birmingham News* (30 June 1989): A9.

Lockhart, James. " 'We Real Cool': Dialect in the Middle-School Classroom." *English Journal* (December 1991): 53–57.

Love, Alice Anne. "Ebonics Taught at Black Psychologists Meeting." *Arizona Republic* (10 August 1997): A13.

Monteith, Mary K. "Implications of the Ann Arbor Decision: Black English and the Reading Teacher." *Journal of Reading* 23 (1980): 556–559.

"New Test for Black English." *New York Times* (August 1979): 1, 5.

"No Easy Way Out: Alabama School Officials Understand Ebonics Is No Shortcut to Fixing Education Problems." *Birmingham News* (27 September 1996): A10. Editorial.

"Oakland Recognizes Black English as Second Language." *Birmingham News* (20 December 1996): A10.

O'Neill, Wayne. "Dealing with Bad Ideas: Twice Is Less." *English Journal* (April 1990): 80–87.

"A Passion for Complex Issues." *Newsweek* (13 January 1997): 21.

Patterson, Nick. "Memo: Missive or Missile? Attempt at Humor Sets Off Racism Debate." *Birmingham News* (22 February 1997): C1.

Peters, Mike. "Cartoon Comments: 'Youz Goin' ta Oakland.' " *Birmingham News* (4 January 1996): A11.

Pitts, Leonard. "Oakland Schools Way Out of Line with Their Black English Decision." *Birmingham News* (27 December 1996): A11.

"Principal Reprimands Volunteer for Questionable Ebonics Assignment." *Birmingham Times* (13 March 1997): A3.

Raspberry, William. "Oakland Officials Haven't Found Magic in Ebonics." *Birmingham News* (3 January 1997): A13.

Rockhill, Rae Ann. "Area Educators Say Move Was Misguided." *Journal and Courier* (22 January 1997): A1–A2.

Royko, Mike. "Review & Comment: When You Talk in Ebonics, You Be Savin' Words." *Birmingham News* (12 January 1997): C6.

"Schools Must Help Break Down the Black English Barriers." *Phi Delta Kappan* (August 1979): 89.

Seymour, Dorothy Z. "Black Children, Black Speech." In William H. Roberts and Gregoire Turgeon, eds., *About Language: A Reader for Writers*. Boston: Houghton Mifflin, 1989, pp. 274–281.

Short, Jasper. "Do You Hear What I Hear?" *Essence* (January 1997): 111.

Smith, Arthur L. *Language, Communication, and Rhetoric in Black America*. New York: Harper and Row, 1972.

Sowell, Thomas. "Origin of Ebonics Fairy Tale Continues." *Birmingham News* (19 January 1997): C3.

Stoller, Paul, ed. *Black American English: Its Background and Its Usage in the Schools and Literature*. New York: Dell, 1975.

Thompson, Dorothy Perry. "From 'It Easy' to 'It IS Easy': Empowering the African-American Student in the Racially Mixed Classroom." *Clearing House* 63 (March 1990): 314–317.

Tucker, Cynthia. "Don't Make Improper English 'a Black Thing.' " *Birmingham News* (5 January 1997): C3.

Whiteman, Marcia Farr. *Reactions to Ann Arbor: Vernacular Black English and Education*. Arlington, VA: Center for Applied Linguistics, 1980.

Winsboro, Betsy L., and Irvin D. Solomon. "Standard English vs. 'The American Dream.' " *Education Digest* (December 1990): 51–52.

Wolfram, Walt, and Nona H. Clarke. *Black/White Speech Relationships*. Washington, DC: Center for Applied Linguistics, 1971.

3

"Women and Chillun and Chickens and Cows": Relations Between Men and Women

Zora Neale Hurston opens *Their Eyes Were Watching God* with what initially seems too simple a premise: that men think and behave one way and women another. In fact, she purposely teases the readers with what seems also to be a statement on *humankind* in general: "Ships at a distance have every *man's* wish on board" (*TEWWG* 1, emphasis added). Yet the last sentence of the first paragraph and the first sentence of the second paragraph point to certain gender dynamics that actually play out in Janie's relationships with Nanny, Logan, Jody, and Tea Cake: "That is the life of men. Now, women forget all those things they don't want to remember, and remember everything they don't want to forget" (*TEWWG* 1). Thus, Hurston establishes the frame of the novel as Janie's story and makes an authorial claim about the fluidity and nonlinearity of women's lives and women's stories. As such, Janie's story winds and weaves with selected details that do not answer the audience's questions about the narrative: Does Janie divorce Logan before running off with and marrying Jody? Does Janie "marry" Tea Cake? Why does Janie devote so little time to her response to Nanny's death? To question Janie's telling of her story is to deny her authority over her own experiences—experiences that define her as a person and a storyteller.

The opening paragraphs also focus the novel on a woman's

story: "So the beginning of this was a woman" (*TEWWG* 1). Echoing and revising biblical scripture—"In the beginning was the Word, and the Word was with God, and the Word was God. He was in the beginning with God" (John 1:1–2)—Hurston affords Janie and Janie's story certain epic proportions while focusing on orality, the spoken Word. Although storytelling rituals specifically and public speaking rituals generally are reserved in western patriarchal cultures for men—black and white—Hurston's novel allows the telling of a woman's story—a black woman's—in her own terms that challenge the illusions of patriarchal order. Janie's is also a life lived beyond patriarchal boundaries and expectations of obedience, passivity, silence, and self-sacrifice. As a black woman's story, it defies European linearity and logic, basing itself instead on possibility and process, not product and certainty.

Janie's story is also that of African American community achieved through talking and testifying. As we witness Janie moving toward personal and spiritual fulfillment, we witness the rigidity and futility of patriarchal efforts to define her order. As Janie tells and retells her story, she also moves across boundaries into spaces traditionally occupied by and for men, spaces that define individual freedom and personal independence for one who dares to think, speak, act, and accept responsibility for her actions.

Yet Hurston blurs lines that would too easily signify men's behavior and women's behavior and values. In the character of Nanny, Hurston contradicts some readers' assertions that the novel is a feminist male-basher. Indeed, because of Nanny's experiences as a former slave, she has come to accept on one level the patriarchal order handed down by white masters. For Nanny, "the white man dumps his load on the black man to carry and the black man dumps his load on the black woman to carry," and "de nigger woman is da mule of the world." (*TEWWG* 29) Whereas Nanny perceives the mule image as a negative, something Janie must work hard not to become, Janie does not accept this negative image of herself. Rather, if she is perceived as a mule by others, it is not Janie's own self-perception. If she is the mule, she is a thinking mule that acts on instinct, not on others' demands. Janie asserts: "Womenfolks thinks sometimes too!" (*TEWWG* 111) Hence, Nanny's efforts to "protect" Janie by marrying her to the older Logan Killicks are frustrating and futile for Janie, as her desire is to explore the world, to take risks, and to savor life's possibilities—all qualities expected of and reserved for men in western cultures.

Consistent throughout the novel are rituals that characterize patriarchal efforts to control women by treating them like children. Jody boldly articulates such sentiments: "Somebody [men] got to think for women and chillun and chickens and cows. [T]hey . . . don't think none theirselves" (*TEWWG* 101). To maintain the illusory order wherein women are passive, silent, and obedient gatekeepers for this order, men often resort to violence. Even Nanny, an embodiment of feminized patriarchy—she values land, property, materialism, ownership, and status—slaps Janie when she encounters Janie's defiance of the prescribed gender role of obedient and patient wife to Logan Killicks. Logan uses violent threats to get Janie to work with the mules, and Jody slaps Janie to demonstrate his manhood and to show curious onlookers that he's the head of his own house. To Nanny, Logan, Jody, and Tea Cake, masculine power is defined by property ownership and possession of obedient women. For Jody specifically, masculine power is embodied in economic gain and sexual prowess. This prowess is snatched from him abruptly and unexpectedly when Janie—after being pelted with a myriad of insults from Jody about her allegedly ungraceful aging—retaliates full-force by attacking the core of his existence as a man; his sexual manhood. "Humph! Talkin' 'bout *me* lookin' old! When you pull down yo' britches, you look lak de change uh life" (*TEWWG* 123). An insult that Jody may have accepted better in a private conversation between himself and Janie becomes, in front of his male peers, a humbling bomb exploding in his face. After this public display of Janie's ability to fight and defend herself with words, Jody dies twice—metaphorically and then shortly thereafter quite literally: "Then Joe Starks realized all the meanings and his vanity bled like a flood. Janie had robbed him of his illusion of irresistible maleness that all men cherish. . . . [W]hat can excuse a man in the eyes of other men for lack of strength?" (*TEWWG* 123) Jody's response to Janie's public impudence is to slap her.

Indeed, Janie's own sexual curiosity and liberation create social havoc for those upholding patriarchal ideals of women's chastity, submissiveness, and social prescription. First, Nanny's personal history as a former slave shows her subjected to the master's sexual whims. Then Leafy is raped by the schoolteacher, and Nanny holds Leafy responsible for a man's violent act of sexual aggression. In Nanny's efforts to "save" and "protect" Janie from moral looseness and social scandal, she can think of only one solution: to marry Janie to a significantly older propertied man with sixty acres and a mule. She tells Janie quite bluntly: "Yeah, Janie, youse got yo' womanhood on yuh. . . . Ah wants to see you married right away" (*TEWWG* 26). The fact that Janie discovers her sexuality from lessons of nature—of bees pollinating flowers as she lies under a pear tree—signals for Hurston a naturalness and an acceptance of women's sexuality, which Janie makes synonymous with "marriage."

Janie's failure to fall in love with Logan Killicks occurs in part because there is no sexual dynamic that attracts Janie to him. He's old, he stinks, and he does not consider Janie an equal partner in the relationship. In fact, when Janie defies his orders, he, like Nanny earlier and Jody later, turns to violence in the form of threats: "Ah'll take holt uh dat ax and come in dere and kill yuh!" (*TEWWG* 53). The fact that Janie leaves Logan is an assertion of her independence, her claim to patriarchal privilege that has traditionally granted men the power to flee the home and to explore the world.

Janie's relationship with Joe Starks (Jody) is at first sexually satisfying until Jody desires to mold her into "de Mayor's wife": "Ah wants to make a wife outa you . . ." (*TEWWG* 50–51). Jody, power-obsessed and with a God-complex signaled in his repetitious "I, god" murmurings, is also insecure about his sexuality and orders Janie to cover her head when he notices other men luxuriating in the sexual possibilities associated with her hair. Janie and Jody's sexual relationship subsequently becomes stale and nonexistent, and her spirit of romance is once again mocked by a patriarchal ideal of order.

With the youngest man, Tea Cake, whom Janie describes as "the love thoughts of women" (*TEWWG* 161), Janie experiences feelings and sensations she recalls from her youthful experience under the pear tree. Her relationship with Tea Cake is initially defined by honesty, trust, partnership, and mutually satisfying sexual play. Tea Cake's masculine identity is not even threatened by Janie's move into the public space of traditional male rituals—going to baseball games, hunting, playing checkers, fishing, and driving a car; he actually introduces her to these rituals and invites her into this space. Yet Tea Cake eventually falls prey to public perception when he feels that his manhood is somehow being undermined. To publicly demonstrate his manhood, he, too, resorts to violence against Janie:

> Before the week was over, [Tea Cake] had whipped Janie. Not because her behavior justified his jealousy, but it relieved that awful fear inside him. Being able to whip her reassured him in possession. No brutal beating at all. He just slapped her about a bit to show he was boss. Everybody talked about it the next day in the fields. It aroused a sort of envy in both men and women. (*TEWWG* 218)

Janie is independent, propertied, and can think for herself. Tea Cake has little more than a charming personality, talent with a guitar, and a desire to make his control over Janie clear to curious onlookers.

The fact that Janie is forty years old and Tea Cake is fifteen years younger is also a source of scandal and curiosity for the gossipy townspeople: "What dat ole forty year ole 'oman doin' wid her hair swingin' down her back lak some young gal?—Where she left dat young lad of a boy she went off here wid?" (*TEWWG* 10). The fact that she leaves with a younger man and returns wearing overalls—traditional male costuming—instead of "that blue satin dress she left here in"—traditional female, upper-class costuming—further symbolizes Janie's move outside of society's expectations for women and men and inside her own self-defined desires as an individual who has seen the horizon for herself. If she still remains to others a "mule of de world," she has for herself defined that mule as strong, resilient, self-sufficient, responsible, defiant, and independent. Hence, Janie as a black woman joins a noble crowd of resilient, risk-taking blues women like Bessie Smith and Billie Holiday who put their hands on their hips, rolled their eyes, and proclaimed their right to do whatever they wanted to do, when they wanted to do it, how they wanted to do it, and with whom they wanted to do it. And as the folks criticized and talked about them, they went about the business of doing their own things.

SOJOURNER TRUTH ON WOMEN'S RIGHTS

The former slave Sojourner Truth presented a speech at a women's rights conference in Akron, Ohio, in 1851. Her now-famous speech, "Woman's Rights," reiterates Zora Neale Hurston's black feminist and womanist presentation of the character Janie Crawford. Although Truth deals with women's rights in particular, her focus is also Hurston's in *Their Eyes Were Watching God*—that any human being should be treated equally with any other human being and that everyone should be granted freedoms of self-definition and self-determination. Notice Truth's preacherly posture as she assumes a public authority traditionally reserved for men. Consider also the impact of dialect as it contributes to both meaning and audience impact. Might Truth's words be the sermon that Nanny wishes she could have preached as a slave? Discuss the significance of the refrain "And a'n't I a woman?" Discuss also the appropriateness or inappropriateness of Truth's attack on patriarchal Christian ideologies.

SOJOURNER TRUTH, "WOMAN'S RIGHTS" (1851)

Wall, chilern, whar dar is so much racket dar must be somethin' out of kilter. I tink dat 'twixt de niggers of de Souf and de womin at de Norf, all talkin' 'bout rights, de white men will be in a fix pretty soon. But what's all dis here talkin' 'bout?

Dat man ober dar say dat womin needs to be helped into carriages and lifted ober ditches, and to hab de best place everywhar. Nobody eber helps me into carriages, or ober mud puddles, or gibs me any best place! And a'n't I a woman? Look at my arm! I have ploughed, and planted, and gathered into barns, and no man could head me! And a'n't I a woman? I could work as much and eat as much as a man—when I could get it—and bear de lash as well! And a'n't I a woman? I have borne thirteen chilern, and seen 'em mos' all sold off to slavery, and when I cried out with my mother's grief, none but Jesus heard me! And a'n't I a woman?

Den dey talks 'bout dis ting in de head; what dis dey call it? ("Intellect," whispered some one near.) Dat's it, honey. What dat got to do wid womin's rights or nigger's rights? If my cup won't hold but a pint, and yourn holds a quart, wouldn't ye be mean not to let me have my little half-measure full?

Den dat little man in black dar, he say women can't have as much rights as men, 'cause Christ wan't a woman! Whar did your Christ come from? Whar did your Christ come from? From God and a woman! Man had nothin' to do wid Him!

If de fust woman God ever made was strong enough to turn de world upside down all alone, dese women togedder (and she glanced her eye over the platform) ought to be able to turn it back, and get it right side up again! And now dey is asking to do it, de men better let 'em.

Words of Fire: An Anthology of African-American Feminist Thought. Ed. Beverly Guy-Sheftall. New York: The New Press, 1995, 36.

TOPICS FOR WRITTEN OR ORAL EXPLORATION

1. Locate and discuss specific passages in the novel that address the roles of men and women.

2. Why does Jody equate women with chickens and cows?

3. Discuss the difference between Nanny's interpretation of the mule image and Hurston's.

4. Discuss Nanny's desire to speak from a public platform as a young woman.

5. How does Nanny's life as a former slave shape her worldview of relationships between men and women as well as race relations between blacks and whites?

6. Discuss Hurston's use of nature imagery to present Janie's sexual awakening.

7. How does Hurston present marriage in the novel?

8. Compare Hurston's presentation of marriage in *Their Eyes Were Watching God* with her presentation of marriage in her short story "Sweat."

9. Does Hurston bash men in order to celebrate women?

10. Discuss Hurston's presentation of heterosexuality without graphic and offensive language.

11. How do social attitudes toward human sexuality differ along gender lines? Is there a double standard in terms of what men and women can think about and say and the way they are expected to behave sexually?

12. Why does Hurston not have Janie experience motherhood?

13. Discuss the significance of Leafy's rape by the schoolteacher. Is the schoolteacher black or white? Does it matter what color the rapist is?

14. Discuss the implications of Nanny's last intimate encounter with Master Robert.

15. To what extent does heterosexuality contribute to the blues motif in the novel?

16. Consider Hurston's presentation of black women's sexuality with various treatments of black women's heterosexuality in such texts as *for colored girls who have considered suicide/when the rainbow is enuf* by Ntozake Shange, *The Color Purple* by Alice Walker, *I Know Why the Caged Bird Sings* by Maya Angelou, and *Beloved* by Toni Morrison. Identify similarities and differences.

17. Locate declarations and celebrations of black women's heterosexuality in the blues songs of such women artists as Billie Holiday, Bessie Smith, Esther Phillips, and Aretha Franklin. Can you identify moments in various songs that parallel Janie's experiences in the novel?

BIBLIOGRAPHY

Angelou, Maya. *I Know Why the Caged Bird Sings*. New York: Bantam, 1969.

———. "Phenomenal Woman." In *And Still I Rise: A Book of Poems*. New York: Random House, 1978.

Atwood, Margaret. "What Is a Woman's Novel? For That Matter, What Is a Man's?" *Ms.* (August 1986): 98.

Bambara, Toni Cade, ed. *The Black Woman: An Anthology*. New York: Penguin, 1970.

Beale, Frances. "Double Jeopardy: To Be Black and Female." In Toni Cade Bambara, ed., *The Black Woman: An Anthology*. New York: Penguin, 1970, pp. 90–100.

Cooper, Priscilla Hancock. "Call Me Black Woman." In *Call Me Black Woman*. Louisville, KY: Doris Publications, 1993, p. 47.

Edward, Sister Ann. "Three Views on Blacks: The Black Woman in American Literature." *College English Association Critic* 37 (May 1975): 14–16.

Evans, Mari. "I Am a Black Woman." In *I Am a Black Woman*. New York: Quill, 1970, pp. 11–12.

Gates, Henry Louis, Jr., ed. *Reading Black, Reading Feminist: A Critical Anthology*. New York: Meridian, 1990.

Giovanni, Nikki. "Nikki Rosa." In Toni Cade Bambara, ed., *The Black Woman: An Anthology*. New York: Penguin, 1970, pp. 15–16.

Guy-Sheftall, Beverly, ed. *Words of Fire: An Anthology of African-American Feminist Thought*. New York: New Press, 1995.

Hull, Gloria T., Patricia Bell Scott, and Barbara Smith, eds. *All the Women Are White, All the Blacks Are Men, But Some of Us Are Brave: Black Women's Studies*. New York: Feminist Press, 1982.

Lincoln, Abbey. "Who Will Revere the Black Woman?" In Toni Cade Bambara, ed., *The Black Woman: An Anthology*. New York: Penguin, 1970, pp. 80–84.

Lindsey, Kay. "The Black Woman as Woman." In Toni Cade Bambara, ed., *The Black Woman: An Anthology*. New York: Penguin, 1970, pp. 85–89.

Morrison, Toni. *Sula*. New York: New American Library, 1982.

Mullen, Bill, ed. *Revolutionary Tales: African-American Women's Short Stories from the First Story to the Present*. New York: Dell, 1995.

Syfers, Judy. "I Want a Wife." In Joseph Trimmer and Maxine Hairston, eds., *Riverside Reader*. Boston: Houghton Mifflin, 1981.

Toomer, Jean. "Avey." In *Cane*. New York: Liveright, 1975, pp. 42–47.

———. "Carma." In *Cane*. New York: Liveright, 1975, pp. 10–11.

———. "Fern." In *Cane*. New York: Liveright, 1975, pp. 14–17.

———. "Karintha." In *Cane*. New York: Liveright, 1975, pp. 1–2.

Truth, Sojourner. "When Woman Gets Her Rights Man Will Be Right." In Beverly Guy-Sheftall, ed., *Words of Fire: An Anthology of African-American Feminist Thought*. New York: New Press, 1995, pp. 37–38.

———. "Woman's Rights." In Beverly Guy-Sheftall, ed., *Words of Fire: An Anthology of African-American Feminist Thought*. New York: New Press, 1995, p. 36.

Walker, Alice. *The Color Purple*. New York: Simon & Schuster, 1985.

4 ———————————————————————

"Find Out If They's White or Black": Race Relations

When *Their Eyes Were Watching God* was published in 1937, there were clear lines separating whites and blacks geographically, socially, and even psychologically. While Hurston doesn't write about black-white race riots or racial violence that later characterized the politically pivotal 1960s, she details a clearly understood and respected code of conduct that kept blacks in their places of alleged inferiority beneath and behind white Americans. These written and unwritten but understood laws—Jim Crow laws—were commandments for Negro survival.[1] Sometimes written—FOR WHITES ONLY—but always clear, these laws extended to all public spaces: hospitals, hotels, housing, swimming pools, parks, public transportation, and even cemeteries. Such codes are vividly depicted by Richard Wright in his ironically titled autobiographical sketch, "The Ethics of Living Jim Crow."[2] They include the following:

> Blacks should not fight whites.
>
> Blacks should not challenge the absolute authority of whites.
>
> White authority is absolute truth.
>
> Blacks should not condescend to whites or present themselves as anything but inferior to whites.
>
> Blacks should not be in certain places after dark.

Blacks should not make efforts to educate themselves with book learning.

Blacks should turn their heads in the face of witnessing white corruption.

Black men should not look lustingly upon white women.

Blacks should always show respect for whites in their presence.

Blacks should always address and answer whites with "Sir" and "Ma'am."

It is not coincidental that these laws are similar in tone and design to the laws that governed slaves in the antebellum South. Indeed, the laws that prevailed during the period of slavery and the subsequent Jim Crow era that lasted until the 1950s and the Civil Rights movement were meant to maintain clearly marked racial boundaries defined and controlled by whites.

In a novel so steeped in feminist and womanist consciousness, it becomes easy to put race relations in a secondary position when in fact *Their Eyes Were Watching God* is grounded in African American experiences related to an awareness of a greater, controlling, and even dangerous white presence looming throughout. Unlike Richard Wright and his brand of social protest manifested through black-white violence, death and suffering, and black male–white male centeredness, Zora Neale Hurston does not focus exclusively or obsessively on the tensions resulting from Jim Crow existence in the South. Rather, Hurston's social protest comes in the form of decentering the white presence in her celebration of the fullness of black existence, a fullness maintained and sustained despite the oppressive political, social, and historical status of black people. White people in the novel are present, but only marginally. Hence, Hurston's colorful characters emerge gracefully and skillfully to take center stage in this black cultural extravaganza. As Sterling Brown astutely notes in his review of the novel, it is about black-white race relations in a very real and unimagined way:

Living in an all-colored town, these people [Hurston's characters] escape the worst pressures of class and caste. There is little harshness, there is enough money and work to go around. The author does not dwell upon the "people ugly from ignorance and broken from being poor" who swarm upon the "muck" for the short-time

Until the 1950s, signs like these were common markers of legally enforced laws of racial segregation in America. Discuss the "rationale" behind such laws. What were they to accomplish in defining and sustaining social order?

jobs. But here is bitterness, sometimes oblique, in the enforced folk manner, and sometimes forthright.[3]

Whereas God didn't Himself design the racial hierarchy that prevails in the South, maintains Hurston, the white folks surely positioned themselves to author such a design.

Hurston's emphasis on black-white race relations occurs at the outset of the novel when she affords a setting for the black porch-sitters to create themselves through talking rituals. It is only after the black workers have completed their tasks as work animals for the white bosses that they are allowed a chance to assemble and redefine their humanity through talk. The white bossman becomes the white people who get to higher ground before the flood and the black people, and he becomes the white guards in charge of burying the dead after the hurricane at the end of the novel. Whereas the fear of the hurricane and deaths resulting from its force have equalized blacks and whites at the moment that "their eyes were watching god" (*TEWWG* 236) and "trying to see beyond seeing" (*TEWWG* 252) in this existential moment, the "burying the dead" ritual afterwards is a reminder that black-white relations are anything but equal. Whites are buried in coffins in whites-only cemeteries, blacks in boxes in the black graveyard. Ordered to "examine every last one of 'em [dead bodies] and find out if they's white or black," Tea Cake voices Hurston's fundamental questioning of the absurdity of Jim Crow: "They's [whites] mighty particular how dese dead folks goes tuh judgment. . . . Look lak dey think God don't know nothin' 'bout de Jim Crow law" (*TEWWG* 254.)

Through Nanny's slave experiences, Hurston addresses American history and African American experience. As a slave woman subjected to the habitual rape—literally and figuratively—by a white master, Nanny's perspective of the world is a direct result of her own life in racial and gender terms: white men are at the top of the social ladder of privilege, black men are beneath white men, and black women are beneath the black men. The white man wields his power over both black men and women; the black man, who cannot challenge or control the white man, can only dump his anger, frustration, and feelings of powerlessness on black women. It is this perspective that Nanny offers to Janie, especially as it relates to the relationship between men and women. Nanny's ideas about race are further evidenced in her perception of her own life with the white Washburns. Somehow for Nanny, any proximity with good white folks makes her better socially. In fact, raising Janie in such close proximity to the white Washburns made Janie unaware of her own blackness. She admits that she didn't realize she was black until she was six years old. This admission does not suggest that Janie wanted to be white; it only stresses the reality that black children learn very early what it means not to be white. Coupled with this lesson of life along racial lines is the lesson Janie receives later from Nanny about women's roles in relation to men's.

Attitudes toward race relations are also addressed in the novel's treatment of intraracism wherein whiteness and white European features are cherished and black Negroid features are lamented. If white equals privilege and advantage, darkness and black are its opposite. Hence, the lighter the skin, the closer black individuals are perceived by both whites and blacks to be more like and pleasing to superior whites. In the character of Mrs. Taylor, who wants blacks to marry light-complexioned blacks to "lighten up de race" (*TEWWG* 209), and whose attitude toward blacks is as racist as any white person's, Hurston attacks this internal divider of community. Hurston shows that with whiteness comes not only economic power and social authority but also aesthetics of beauty, as "Mrs. Turner, like all other believers had built an altar to the unattainable—Caucasian characteristics for all. . . . So she didn't cling to Janie Woods the woman. She paid homage to Janie's Caucasian characteristics—her luxurious straight-hair, thin-lips, high nose, and coffee-and-cream complexion" (*TEWWG* 208, 216). Even Janie's identity as a mulatto—Janie's mother, Leafy, was the product of Nanny's forced sexual submission to a white master—reminds us that black-white race relations are not secondary to the novel.

The emphasis on black-white reductions of life experiences under the rule of Jim Crow resurfaces in Janie's murder trial at the novel's end. With white men in authority to determine Janie's life—a white male judge and twelve white male jurors—Hurston revisits Nanny's worldview as a former slave. As the whites are seated in the front of the courtroom, the "powerless" blacks are herded and stand in the rear itching for a chance to testify against

Janie, to make themselves human in a world where they lack power and authority. Only the testimony of the white doctor convinces the jury that Janie did not commit first-degree murder in her deliberate shooting of Tea Cake. As black powerlessness is manifested in silence in this instance, Hurston declares speech once again as the sign of humanness and authority over oneself: "They [blacks attending the trial] were there with their tongues cocked and loaded, the only real weapon left to weak folks . . . in the presence of white folks" (*TEWWG* 275).

Many have criticized Hurston for presenting whites too sympathetically in the novel and for not presenting direct racial confrontation and violence. In fact, there is ambivalence regarding white people in the details that the whites side with Janie in the trial whereas the blacks make a judgment of guilty without just cause. The blacks even turn the trial into a black-white issue, insisting that had Janie killed a white person, she would have been found guilty and put in jail:

> "Aw you know dem white mens wuzn't gointuh do nothin' tuh no woman dat look lak her."
> "She didn't kill no white man, did she? Well, long as she doesn't shoot no white man she kin kill jus' as many niggers as she please."
> (*TEWWG* 280)

NOTES

1. See C. Vann Woodward, *The Strange Career of Jim Crow* (New York: Oxford University Press, 1966). Woodward explains that the connection between the mocked black slave character by T. D. Rice in the 1800s through time became a symbol of marked black and white racial separation. Such laws were to keep blacks in an oppressed social and political position allegedly below whites who created and policed the laws for black behavior.

2. Richard Wright, "The Ethics of Living Jim Crow," in *Uncle Tom's Children* (New York: Harper & Row, 1989), 3–15.

3. Sterling Brown, review of *Their Eyes Were Watching God*, in Henry Louis Gates Jr. and A. K. Appiah, eds., *Zora Neale Hurston: Critical Perspectives Past and Present* (New York: Amistad, 1993), 20–21.

TOPICS FOR WRITTEN OR ORAL EXPLORATION: JIM CROW

1. Research the origins of character Jim Crow.
2. Research the connection between Jim Crow minstrel songs and the Jim Crow character.

3. How does Hurston define white identity in the novel?

4. What components constitute African American cultural identity in the novel?

5. What does it mean to be African American in a predominantly white American society?

6. To what extent does black-white racial segregation exist in the 1990s?

7. Does Hurston distinguish between African American culture and southern culture?

8. Look at President Clinton's "Initiative on Race." It was instituted by President Clinton in June 1997. It is intended to open a national dialogue on multi-racial issues. Clinton appointed a seven-member advisory board, headed by African American historian John Hope Franklin, to counsel him on race relations policies. Also, he conducted monthly town hall meetings across the country. To what extent are the issues presented similar to and different from Hurston's presentation in the novel?

SUGGESTED READINGS ON JIM CROW EXPERIENCES

Angelou, Maya. *I Know Why the Caged Bird Sings*. New York: Bantam, 1988.

Childress, Alice. "Florence." *Masses and Mainstream* 3 (October 1950): 34–47.

Du Bois, W.E.B. "Of the Coming of John." In *The Souls of Black Folk*, in *Three Negro Classics*. New York: Avon Books, 1965, pp. 363–377.

———. "On the Black Belt." In *The Souls of Black Folk*, in *Three Negro Classics*. New York: Avon Books, 1965, pp. 284–301.

Fineman, Howard. "Race: Redrawing the Color Lines." *Newsweek* (29 April 1996): 34–35.

Hacker, Andrew. *Two Nations: Black and White, Separate, Hostile, Unequal*. New York: Charles Scribner's Sons, 1992.

Hughes, Langston. *The Return of Simple*. New York: Hill and Wang, 1994.

———. "A Toast to Harlem." In *The Best of Simple*. New York: Hill and Wang, 1990, pp. 20–23.

Toomer, Jean. "Blood-Burning Moon." In *Cane*. New York: Liveright, 1975, pp. 28–35.

———. "Kabnis." In *Cane*. New York: Liveright, 1975, pp. 81–116.

Woodward, C. Vann. *The Strange Career of Jim Crow*. New York: Oxford University Press, 1966.

Wright, Richard. *Uncle Tom's Children*. New York: Harper and Row, 1989.

INTRARACISM IN *THEIR EYES WERE WATCHING GOD*

Zora Neale Hurston knew how ingrained discrimination based on light and dark skin was within African American communities. She also knew how divisive this discrimination was within black communities. Intraracism is based on skin hues, where light-skinned persons were treated better and thought to be more privileged than dark-complexioned black people. The fact that lighter-skinned black people were more easily identified as having white ancestry created a racism that further supported the mythology that white was the ideal and anything close to white was definitely better than something closer to black.

Hurston introduces the divisiveness of internal discrimination through the character of Mrs. Turner, whose racial self-hatred is almost caricatured as compared to Janie's complete identification with blackness despite her mulatto ancestry. Mrs. Turner's desire to have Janie romantically involved with her light-skinned brother reveals the deep-seated intraracial rules involving lightening the race. Although she is not a member of the Blue Veins Society—an organization of blacks so light that their veins show under their skin—Mrs. Turner also reveals a distinct class association with skin gradations.

In this autobiographical and testimonial piece, Bertice Berry details her immediate experience with intraracism. The cultural ignorance of white people in part has led to the perpetuation of racist myths that continue to define aesthetics of African American attractiveness. Compare Berry's commentary to Hurston's presentation of Mrs. Turner as well as Janie's and Berry's own self-definitions of beauty. Does Berry inadvertently set up a critically problematic polarity between light and dark African Americans in the last section of the essay?

BERTICE BERRY, "VISION OF BLACK BEAUTY SHADED BY COLORISM" (1991)

I grew up hearing and accepting that if you were light you were all right, brown you could stick around, but if you were black, you had to get back.

I jumped rope to this ditty and somehow, these not-so-innocent words jumped right off my lips into my head and found their way to my heart.

Other images also found their way there. Images of good hair, pretty light skin, straight noses, skinny thighs and butts.

No matter how hard I prayed, these treasures eluded me.

I was told by my family that I should marry someone light, so my children wouldn't be "too dark." I'd sit for hours trying to determine how dark was too dark.

Who knew? Better yet, who decided? I'd watch television and pick up magazines, hoping to see someone who looked like me being called beautiful.

I saw myself there briefly in the late '60s, but then things returned to "normal," and that "normal" standard of beauty came back. And it didn't include me.

The harder I looked, the more invisible/ugly I became.

In my own arrogance I decided that since I would/could not change myself (bleaching creams, tinted contact lenses and blond hair were out of the question), I had to change the model.

I would broaden the perspective and place myself in it.

I rejected my Barbie doll (her butt was too small, her chest too large and her waist completely out of proportion) and all the other ideas of what was beautiful.

I had new standards: my own.

But I quickly found that thinking positively only works if the people around you think in the same direction.

I decided to work smart.

For two years, I conducted my Ph.D. dissertation research on colorism, that is, prejudicial or preferential treatment by people of the same race toward each other on the basis of skin color.

I believed that not only was colorism alive in the African-American community, it was so internalized that it could be taken as a given.

My investigation led to stories of African-American social clubs and even churches whose memberships were based in part on the applicants' skin color.

The research uncovered a stratification within the community based on color that had social and economic effects.

In an attempt to get some sense of hope, I conducted in-depth interviews with African-American teenagers.

Much to my dismay, they confirmed the hypothesis that more "European" features were preferred and perceived as "better."

I attempted to discuss the phenomenon in formal and informal settings.

Scholars and lay people alike informed me that I was seeing and saying too much.

Some pointed out that colorism was caused by the slave owners' separation of African-Americans, with lighter slaves working in or near the house and darker slaves in the fields and in more "manual" labor.

Therefore, they concluded, the discussion of colorism should only receive a footnote in the chapter on racism.

Some argued that people who accepted Euro-standards were not trying to be European, just more beautiful.

I'm still confused by this argument.

Others thought it would be best to let sleeping dogs lie.

But the dogs keep barking.

African-Americans continue to discriminate on the basis of skin color and European features.

We still speak in terms of good and bad hair.

We often believe that lighter blacks are arrogant, stuck-up and should not be trusted, while their darker sisters are lazy and low-class.

Young men still search for the pretty red bone girl.

Women still write to magazines and swap ideas on how to make their children lighter, less African, and we still ignore the issue.

We as African-Americans must take action toward the demise of colorism.

Because the behavior is learned, we can hope that it also can be unlearned.

We must take the responsibility for our actions past and present, and openly recognize our colorist attitudes so that we can begin to alter them.

As a community, African-Americans need to reject the media's limited presentation of "us."

The Vanessa Williams type needn't be the dominant role model for our young.

We can and must also admire the Alfre Woodards and Whoopi Goldbergs—those people who look like us.

We can encourage our children to be and love themselves.

We need to go back to a time when we said out loud that we were black and proud, a time when we discovered that big noses were beautiful and nappy hair glorious.

We must teach our children that their uniqueness is to be praised.

We must do that by praising them ourselves.

Birmingham News, 17 November 1991, p. E2.

In "Playing Favorites with Tone of Skin," Roderick Hicks expresses the pain associated with African Americans discriminating against other African Americans on both sides of the colorism rift. Notice how personal choices are controlled by individuals' awareness of skin tone preferences. Colorism is the unspoken dialogue that often determines African Americans' choices in friendship, romance, and marriage. The issue of colorism is further complicated by the relativity of such loaded perceptions of "light" and "dark."

RODERICK HICKS, "PLAYING FAVORITES WITH TONE OF SKIN"
(1993)

Jeanette Wells was adored by her elementary school teachers who gave her preferential treatment.

She passed out class papers and ran errands—activities that usually elevated students to a level of prestige envied by classmates.

She hated it.

Mrs. Wells, who is black, said she received the special attention because of her light skin complexion. She was teased and ridiculed by classmates who knew that was the reason for her higher status.

"I grew up during that time when the (black-is-beautiful) movement was really happening," said Mrs. Wells, now 41. "You try your best to blend in."

Her experiences led her to decide early at least one characteristic of her future husband—dark skin. Jessie Wells, her husband of 21 years, had that characteristic and several others that she liked, she said.

"I wanted someone dark so my kids can be darker than me" said Mrs. Wells, who has three children, all darker than she is. "I didn't want them to go through what I went through."

The skin complexion of American blacks has had a social significance within the race since the days of slavery.

And, though civil rights leaders have for years argued that skin color should not matter, many blacks today acknowledge that the shading of skin remains an important factor in the black community, particularly in social situations such as dating and marriage.

This "colorism" may seem paradoxical. But, for years, American society made color the overriding issue in the lives of blacks. So even now, with slavery and most types of segregation relegated to history, many blacks find it difficult to rid themselves of a preoccupation with color.

Although skin complexion appears to be an insignificant factor in workplace discrimination, many blacks, both dark-skinned and light-skinned, concede that the shading does appear to make a difference in social activities.

"It seems to me that my dark-skinned friends have light-skinned wives," said Oliver Robinson, who is dark and has a light-skinned wife,

Sakina. "Looking at the in-laws, it's the same thing. I don't know if opposites attract or what."

Opposites apparently do attract, at least sometimes.

While light-skinned blacks sometimes seek out darker mates to validate their blackness in the eyes of other blacks, darker-skinned blacks sometimes seek out lighter-skinned mates because they perceive them as being more beautiful, said University of Alabama at Birmingham history professor Horace Huntley.

But favoring lighter-skinned blacks over blacks with darker shades today is politically incorrect and many blacks would not publicly admit it, Huntley said.

There was less of a social stigma on such behavior in the 1960's, prior to the black pride movement catching on, Huntley said.

"The lighter the person was, the better one was treated and the lighter the girl, the more preferable," Huntley said.

David Points, 75, who has a light skin complexion, said he noticed as a young man that he often was treated better than darker-skinned blacks by whites and fellow blacks.

His Air Force buddies told him they preferred light-skinned women because they were nicer and that darker-skinned women "would cuss you out," said Points, who is married to a dark-skinned woman, Clemmie.

Points said he got an easier job at the U.S. Postal Service after requesting it, although he thought some of his darker colleagues were more qualified or had more seniority. And if he was in a group with other blacks, white travelers who needed directions would direct their questions to him.

Older blacks said having dark skin sometimes kept you off of the high school cheerleading squad, out of consideration for stage performances and out of some black social clubs and black colleges.

Blacks wanting to be accepted by some of these organizations had to pass the "brown bag test" in which their skin was compared to the color of the bag. If their skin was lighter, they were accepted.

Josephine C. Marshall said she was at the head of her class academically in the 1930's at what is now Parker High School. But she said the school disqualified her from participating in some extracurricular activities because of her dark skin.

"But it didn't work at Tuskegee Institute—thank God for that. It was based on your grades," Mrs. Marshall said.

Helen George Heath, who attended Parker at the same time as Mrs. Marshall, said she and some other dark-skinned students escaped denial into school activities because their parents were ministers or professionals. Her father, Rev. Charles Henry George, was a well-known church pastor.

Tequila Barron, a light-skinned 21-year-old biology student at Miles College, said some of her dark male friends have told her that they were afraid to approach her because they assumed she only wanted to associate with light-skinned guys.

To some degree, dark skin is again fashionable, if models in magazine ads and popular movie actors can be used as a guide. Actor Wesley Snipes, the star of such movies as "Jungle Fever" and "Demolition Man," is dark and is one of today's most popular actors.

"Dark-skinned brothers (today) are more appearance-conscious, more educated and more aware of world society," said Randall Jermaine, 33, who is dark. "All of these things together attract all different types of females. It's the 'in' thing right now."

But some dark-skinned women say they are not a part of this revived fashion. Darker-skinned women are increasingly seeking out lighter-skinned mates to father their children in hopes that the children will be lighter and avoid some of the prejudices they experienced, Maryland writer Portia Williams wrote in an April *Washington Post* column.

"If you're black, the struggle is hard enough. But if you're 'too black,' it can become your life," Ms. Williams wrote.

There is a belief by some, however, that overall, complexion is becoming less important among blacks.

Michelle Wallace, president of the Black Student Awareness Committee at UAB, said black students mingling on campus appear to do it without regard to complexion.

She credits the growing popularity of Afrocentrism—interest in Africa and African-inspired culture. "I think black people are more in touch with their Afrocentrism, so it's OK to be brown-skinned," said Ms. Wallace, who is dark.

Birmingham Post-Herald, 30 October 1993, p. C1.

In this essay, Roderick Hicks offers a historical context for the color discriminations among African Americans. Hicks explains slavery and black-white race mixing or interracial pairings that produced biracial offspring as sources of intraracist perceptions and mythologies that persist in the minds and practices of blacks even today. Such attention to and discrimination based on light and dark skin hues are informed by western European ideologies associating black with negativity and ugliness, and white with positivity, goodness, and all that is right with the world.

RODERICK HICKS, "BIAS HAS ROOTS IN AMERICAN HISTORY"
(1993)

Subtly lingering in some black social circles is an issue many blacks are embarrassed to admit.

Some will deny it.

But for centuries, there have been American blacks, with their wide spectrum of skin shadings, who used complexion as a basis of intraracial bias.

Historians say this phenomenon, termed "colorism" by author Alice Walker, has its roots in American slavery.

Lighter-skinned slaves were given the preferred house duties, while darker-skinned blacks tilled the soil under the sweltering Southern sun.

"This is part of the legacy of slavery," said University of Alabama at Birmingham history professor Horace Huntley. "The slave masters made one feel better than the other. They needed that division to control those in the fields."

Over the generations, the idea that light is the preferred skin complexion became engrained in the American psyche, Huntley said. Whites believed it. Light-skinned blacks believed it. And dark-skinned blacks believed it.

"They internalized this idea," Huntley said. "When it comes to race, logic tends to leave."

White people who went to Africa 300 years ago to bring slaves back to the New World had sex with the blacks on the slave ships, producing children, said Miles College history professor Bandele Thomas.

Back home in America, those offspring mated with both blacks and whites, creating even more shades of people, Thomas said. All of the offspring were considered black and most were enslaved.

The slaves with the lightest skin and most European features such as thin lips and soft, straight hair were treated better.

"They resembled them (slave owners) in some respect," Thomas said. "Those with lighter skin could sometimes get their freedom faster. Some got to go to school and to own businesses. . . . The whites told the blacks that the light-skinned were smarter."

Since lighter-skinned blacks had more advantages than darker-skinned blacks, it is understandable that the earliest prominent black Americans typically were light-skinned, Huntley said. Their prominence perpetuated the notion that light is good and dark is bad, Huntley said.

"In effect, it confirmed for many that the lighter you were, the better off one would become," Huntley said.

Certain words and phrases and some popular sayings also contributed, Huntley said. Many of these equated light and white with good, and dark and black with bad.

"When someone dies, you go to the funeral in black," Huntley said. "When you marry, you get married in white. The devil's food is chocolate but angel food is lighter."

Africa and African features also were cast negatively, he said. Africa was called the "dark continent" and talked about as an uncivilized, savage place. Broad noses, coarse hair, full lips and other African features were depicted as unattractive.

Complexion played an increasing role in the black community over the decades. Some black colleges denied admission to darker-skinned blacks and some social clubs, including Greek-letter organizations, favored lighter-skinned applicants.

Helen George Heath said she believes she was one of the most popular teachers at Parker High School in the 1940's, '50s and '60s because she did not give special attention to light-skinned students as several other teachers did.

In some classrooms, teachers called mostly on light-skinned students to answer class questions, and in some classrooms students were segregated according to skin complexion, she said.

A movement that attacked the negative images of African heritage and dark skin started about the 1920's when Marcus Garvey advocated black Americans returning to Africa to start their own country. The Nation of Islam, a religious organization of black Muslims, was visible in the 1960's for promoting blackness as a positive. Later in the 1960's, the black power movement caught on.

Blacks were increasingly celebrating their blackness while fighting for equal rights.

"There was a lot of self-esteem established . . . when blacks realized they had a lot to offer to the total world," Mrs. Heath said. "We began to realize our potential."

There appears to be a resurfacing of black pride in the United States today—Afrocentric books, clothing, artwork and hair styles are in vogue.

But skin complexion issues continue to be debated within the race. Spike Lee dealt with the issue in his films "School Daze," "Mo' Better Blues" and "Jungle Fever." In "Jungle Fever," a dark-skinned man with a light-skinned wife had an affair with a white woman.

But blacks have come a long way in dealing with this issue and finally, whites are acknowledging black beauty, Huntley said. Some whites are altering their own features to acquire African features, such as darker skin, full lips and bigger breasts and hips, Huntley said.

"The beauty standard is being redefined," he said.

Birmingham Post-Herald, 30 October 1993, p. C1.

TOPICS FOR WRITTEN OR ORAL EXPLORATION:
INTRARACISM

1. Outline the racist myths presented in Mrs. Turner's efforts to pair Janie with her light-complected brother.

2. Look at pictures of African Americans in magazines for patterns of favoritism toward those with light skin.

3. Look at images of African Americans on television to determine if the bias toward skin color is apparent.

4. Examine references to the skin tone of African Americans in popular music.

5. Discuss the references to the skin tone of African Americans in popular music of the past as noted by cultural critic Lawrence W. Levine in his book *Black Culture and Black Consciousness: Afro-American Folk Thought from Slavery to Freedom* (New York: Oxford University Press, 1978), 284–292.

6. Discuss the connections between racism, intraracism, and passing [black individuals, usually racially mixed, whose skin is light enough that they allow themselves to be perceived as white in order to have access to white advantages].

7. Research the history of slaves' treatment by their masters as determined by the lightness or darkness of the slaves' skin.

8. Survey the popular models of today for patterns in colorism. Is there a balance between light- and dark-skinned models?

9. Discuss the relativity of the terms *light* and *dark* in terms of skin hues.

10. Look up the words *black* and *white* in a dictionary. How many negative ideas are associated with the word *black*? How many positive associations with the word *black*? How many negative associations with the word *white*? How many positive associations with the word *white*?

SUGGESTED READINGS ON INTRARACISM

Bates, Karen Grigsby. "The Color Thing." *Essence* (September 1994): 79–80, 132, 134–135.

Berry, Bertice. "Vision of Black Beauty Shaded by Colorism." *Birmingham News* (17 November 1991): E2.

Cose, Ellis. "One Drop of Bloody History." *Newsweek* (13 February 1995): 70, 72.

Davis, Ossie. "The English Language Is My Enemy!" *Negro History Bulletin* 30 (April 1967): 18.

Gillespie, Marcia Ann. "Mirror Mirror." *Essence* (January 1993): 73–74, 96.

Hicks, Roderick. "Bias Has Roots in American History." *Birmingham News/Birmingham Post-Herald* (30 October 1993): C1.

———. "Playing Favorites with Tone of Skin." *Birmingham News/Birmingham Post-Herald* (30 October 1993): C1.

Hopkins, Tracy E. "Seeing Colors." *Seventeen* (December 1993): 70.

Hughes, Langston. "Harlem Sweeties." In *Shakespeare in Harlem*. New York: Alfred A. Knopf, 1945, p. 20.

———. "Passing." In *The Ways of White Folks: Stories by Langston Hughes*. New York: Vintage, 1962, pp. 51–55.

Hurston, Zora Neale. *Color Struck*. In Kathy A. Perkins, ed., *Black Female Playwrights: An Anthology of Plays before 1950*. Bloomington: Indiana University Press, 1989, pp. 89–102.

"Intraracism." *Donahue* (11 February 1988). Cincinnati, OH: Multimedia Entertainment, Incorporated, 11 February 1988. Transcript 021188.

"Intra-Racism." *The Oprah Winfrey Show* (12 May 1987). New York: Journal Graphics Incorporated, 12 May 1997. Transcript #W172.

Larsen, Nella. *Passing*. New York: Penguin, 1997.

"Light vs. Darker-Skinned Women: Do Some Black Men Have a Preference?" *EM* (March 1992): 46–47.

Marriott, Michel. "Colorstruck." *Essence* (November 1991): 57–58, 118, 122.

———. "Light-Skinned Men: Problems and Privileges." *Essence* (November 1988): 75–76, 133–134.

Morganthau, Tom. "What Color Is Black?" *Newsweek* (13 February 1995): 63–65.

Porter, Benita. *Colorstruck*. Bronx, NY: Colorstruck, 1990.

Russell, Kathy, Midge Wilson, and Ronald Hall. *The Color Complex: The Politics of Skin Color among African Americans*. New York: Doubleday, 1993.

Samuels, Allison. "Black Beauty's New Face." *Essence* (24 November 1997): 68.

Sandler, Kathe. *The Question of Color: Healing Racism's Hidden Wounds*. San Francisco: Resolution Incorporated/California Newsreel, 1993. Video cassette.

Thurman, Wallace. *The Blacker the Berry*. . . . New York: Macmillan, 1970.

"Why Skin Color Suddenly Is a Big Issue Again." *Ebony* (March 1992): 120–122.

Wright, Sheryl. "Learning to Cherish My Beauty." *Essence* (February 1997): 40.

INTERVIEWS WITH ANSWERS, ANSWERS AS STORIES

In many ways Zora Neale Hurston presents Janie Crawford's story as an interview, a question-and-answer session with her best friend, Phoeby, as the questioner/interviewer/audience and Janie as the answerer/interviewee/storyteller. When Janie returns to town after being tried and acquitted for the murder of Tea Cake, she is "interviewed" by Phoeby about the events that have brought them back together after so many years. Although the question/inquiry format allows Janie to tell her story, some readers question Hurston's need to have Janie start with childhood recollections. If Phoeby is her best friend, many ask, wouldn't Phoeby already know about Janie's experiences with the Washburn family and about Janie's relationship with Nanny? Nevertheless, the fact that Phoeby (who may or may not be the porch-sitting gossipers' messenger or newscarrier from Janie) gives Janie the opportunity to take center stage and tell her story, which then becomes the narrative of all the other characters and personalities that have defined her experiences.

More broadly speaking, readers might think of *Their Eyes Were Watching God* as Hurston's response to the question: What was life like in the 1930s and 1940s for black people in the South? The novel then is seen as a series of responses that comment on black-white race relations from slavery to Jim Crow and of life lived in the spaces between and around race relations—life experiences of people who are not always focused on the race issue. The following interviews further contextualize the lives of southern blacks who lived during the period when *Their Eyes Were Watching God* was written and published. Each interview constitutes a series of stories and narratives that move from the interviewees' intimately personal details to the interviewees' overtly political commentaries on American society.

The following questions were used to structure the two original interviews conducted by the author for this casebook on *Their Eyes Were Watching God*. Such questions might be used by students to document the stories of elders who also lived during the period when Hurston produced this novel. In comparing these questions with those actually asked and answered (as shown in the interview transcripts), notice that the interviewees' responses often become short narratives. Students should realize that an interview may be conversational and that the purpose of an interview is to hear and document another's stories. As such, an interviewer need not be overly concerned with rigid adherence to a certain ordering of questions or to exact questions. Some questions may blend with others and some questions may be omitted altogether, depending on the nature of the responses from the interviewee. When the interview has been completed, it is important that the interviewer do very little in terms of editing or "correcting" it when transcribing. Only changes regarding readability and clarity should be made. Realize that a crucial part of the interview process is to re-create the story as it is being told. An interviewer should not editorialize or rewrite the interviewee's stories from the interviewer's perspective or with the interviewer's personal biases.

INTERVIEW QUESTIONS

1. What is your full name? Is there any family history behind your name? Who named you? Were you named after anyone in particular? Did/Do you have a nickname or pet name that family and friends call you?

2. How old are you? When were you born? Where were you born?

3. Who were your parents? Where were they born? Were/Are you married? Who was/is your spouse? Where was your spouse born? Describe your wedding. What was life like for a married black couple during the 1920s and 1930s? Do you have any children? Who are they and what are their ages? Do they still live in the South? Do you have any grandchildren? How many? Do you have any great-grandchildren? How many?

4. What was life like for blacks in the South during the 1920s and 1930s?

5. What was life like for black women during the 1920s and 1930s?

6. Describe relations between blacks and whites during the 1920s and 1930s.

7. Was life significantly different for blacks in the South and blacks in other parts of the country?

8. Is most of your family still in the South today?

9. Do you know friends and family who left the South and migrated north in the 1920s and 1930s? Why did they leave the South? Did you ever consider leaving the South?

10. What were the Jim Crow laws? What, in your opinion, was the purpose of these laws? Who created these laws? How were they communicated to blacks? Did the laws seem equally applied to black men and black women?

11. Describe your most vivid Jim Crow experience(s).

12. How did your family respond to the Jim Crow laws?

13. Do you recall any instances of violence against blacks by whites during the 1920s and 1930s? Describe them.

14. What kinds of educational opportunities were available for blacks during the 1920s and 1930s?

15. What kinds of educational opportunities were available for whites during the 1920s and 1930s?

16. What kinds of educational, political, and social opportunities were available for black women during the 1920s and 1930s?

17. Was there a lot of porch-sitting among black southerners during the 1920s and 1930s?

18. What did black folk talk about during the 1920s and 1930s?

19. What were common pastimes for blacks during the 1920s and 1930s?

20. What was it like to be a parent and a mother during the 1920s and 1930s?

21. What role did the church and religion play in the lives of blacks during the 1920s and 1930s?

22. In your opinion, what are the most significant changes in the lives of blacks and black women since the 1920s and 1930s?

23. Is there anything else you want to add that will help young students understand your life and the lives of other blacks and other black women during the 1920s and 1930s?

NOTE: Please record date and time of interview at start of interview. Repeat if interview is not conducted in its entirety in one sitting.

I (*Neal Lester*) know Mr. Joseph Henderson from the church we both attended in Birmingham, Alabama—Grant Chapel African Methodist Episcopal—from about 1986–1994. Mr. Henderson is well respected in his church community as one who is honest, upright, and fair. He agreed to this interview without hesitation, and it was conducted at his home in East Lake (Birmingham, Alabama). While Mr. Henderson offers vivid details of his personal life in the deep South, his narrative reveals the broader experiences of other southern blacks. His interview tells of his own youthful defiance of white dominance, detailing the boundaries of black-white racial segregation, black intimidation and violence from the white supremacist Ku Klux Klan, blacks' economic plights during the 1920s and 1930s, family relations, the role of the church in black families' lives, black-white race relations—both amiable and threatening—family rituals, parent-child relationships, blacks' recreation, entertainment, and music.

INTERVIEW WITH JOSEPH HENDERSON, CONDUCTED AT HIS
HOME IN BIRMINGHAM, ALABAMA (JUNE 21, 1996)

LESTER: How long have you lived in the South?

HENDERSON: In the South, I've practically been everywhere, but I haven't been to California.

LESTER: Oh, okay.

HENDERSON: Wherever the army sends you, that's where you go. I was in World War II.

LESTER: Tell me your full name now.

HENDERSON: Joseph Henderson.

LESTER: Were you named after anybody in particular?

HENDERSON: My grandfather, my mother's father.

LESTER: His name was?

HENDERSON: Joseph Green.

LESTER: Did you have a nickname or a pet name?

HENDERSON: No, everybody just called me Joe.

LESTER: Just called you Joe. How old are you?

HENDERSON: Eighty-six, this past February.

LESTER: That means you were born in . . .

HENDERSON: 1910. I was born 2–10–20, February 20, 1910.

LESTER: Where were you born?

HENDERSON: I was born out from Montgomery [Alabama]. It's a place they called MaGee's Switch. I was born out from MaGee's Switch, a little town like. It ain't there, but that's where I was born. I left or rather my parents moved away from there. I must have been about three or four and we moved to Dollar Cedar out here by Boaz [Alabama], a little old place called Dollar Cedar. That's where my daddy moved, but my uncle he lived over here and eventually got us a house. When I say over here, I mean on the southside [of Birmingham]. I don't mean out here in East Lake. But you [blacks] weren't allowed to walk through here.

LESTER: Oh really?

HENDERSON: Nobody but somebody like me who had a pocket full of bricks as a [black] boy and three or four other [black] boys with me. We might come through here. We were looking for trouble.

LESTER: Now was this a white section?

HENDERSON: Yeah. It was a white section. And right there on 1st Avenue going across on 38th or 39th Street. I believe it's 39th Street. White folks wouldn't allow you to walk through there, young whites. Well, the old folks did too, else they wouldn't be doing it. That's mostly what happened, all them low down things like they still are happening. [White] people still teaching their children they better than blacks, and blacks supposed to do whatever they tell them. All that kind of stuff. I've heard them say, "Well we'll get the Ku Klux out on you," like if I got a little out of line. I saw—I don't know his name, but all of us children called him Mr. Doc; his name was Doc something. I don't know. The rent man come up there. Didn't nobody own no houses hardly, just a very few blacks. Poor folks just didn't own houses, not blacks nor whites. He come up there between 29th and 30th Street, and 5th Avenue South. Black people lived in that alley; they didn't all live like I'm living here. I lived in the alley. A lot of people lived in the alley. The lady didn't have the rent and if you didn't have the rent, they usually set your things out on the street.

LESTER: Oh really?

HENDERSON: Yeah, set them outdoors, out on the street. "If you don't have my money when I come back here," what he was gone do was set her things out. She was afraid. You know you don't want your things setting out and ain't got nowhere to go, to put your stuff. If it rained, it rained on it, and once it rained on all your furniture, it's terrible. I couldn't never stand that. After I got a certain age, my mother died when I was real young. Well, my father married again. Papa married a lady. She had three children and she didn't want him to do nothing for us. And I wasn't used to that, you know because . . . I'd put my Papa up against anybody. Papa was a good man. He said, whatever he said, he would do. Sometimes I might say, "Papa, you gone get me some skates?" But you see there was a house full of us.

LESTER: How many?

HENDERSON: It was thirteen of us. My mother had thirteen children.

LESTER: She had thirteen and he had three from his new wife?

HENDERSON: They didn't live with us. If they had lived with us that would have made us get a piece of the pie. They had their house and we had ours. It was thirteen of us. When he left, one of my sisters was married. The other sister, I don't think you ever saw her. She was a member of Grant Chapel, an evangelist. She was a member of Grant Chapel for years and years. Well, that's why I went to Grant Chapel. That's where all my people were. My parents belonged there and children did whatever parents said do. You couldn't do like they do now. They tell you to do one thing and they do another. They wouldn't have that. We, all my family, all my sisters and brothers went to Grant Chapel. Some particular times, they [Ku Klux Klan] throw around pamphlets on the street, like they throw around these old grocery flyers. They would say, "Be off the street tonight by 9:00 or 8:00," or whatever time they wanted you off. Be off! That wasn't no joke. If you didn't be off, they would be riding in cars with them long white robes with them eyes cut out of them.

LESTER: And the hoods on?

HENDERSON: Yeah, they had hoods on. They would talk. That thing [flyer] would tell you what you were supposed to do. Mostly, as far as I can remember. They would mostly tell you to be off the street and all black folks would be off the street. There might be somebody walking out there, but black folks were mostly off. If you didn't be off the street, Ku Klux will get you. And ain't no telling what the Ku Klux will do to you.

LESTER: And nobody wanted to find out?

HENDERSON: No, no they'd beat you.

LESTER: Were you a teenager during this time?

HENDERSON: Yeah, I can remember then my brother-in-law, my oldest sister's husband, went to the army and came back home in 1919. Well, I was 9. I remember a whole lot of things before I was 9 years old. I spent most of my time at the golf club.

LESTER: Which golf club was that?

HENDERSON: Birmingham Country Club, it was right there now called Highland Park. But that was Birmingham Country Club. I went there when I got out of school. I went in the morning before school. Some [white] golfer would say, "Be up there in the morning at 5:00," and he'd go up there by himself and practice. Then you'd go up there to get the balls. There would be a lot of us [black boys] up there on that street near the bus line every morning. I usually went there mostly by appointment. But somebody would say, "Need you up there in the morning, Joe, for practice." And I'd say, "Yes sir." It was important that you go up there. It was very little money and we needed the money. All poor folks need their money, and we would go up there and caddy. And then I'd run back home and get ready and go to school. I was going to Thomas School.

LESTER: And none of the little white boys caddied?

HENDERSON: We had very few. We had some that were around. A lot of other poor whites say ugly things about them. If you had any close associations with blacks, other than if you worked for them. Well, your mother or your sister, that's fortunate. My mother didn't grow up to work for whites, but my sister did. They went to work for this white lady and that white lady. I mean, I believe all of them at one time or another went to work for white people. And my sister that reared us had worked out there in Mount Calvary. And she had a job. She worked for a pretty nice group of people. They talked the talk like you hear them black folks say, "Before the end of time, the bar rail is gone be on top." So, she kind of feared that. I could tell the way she acted. I would go up there and cut the grass, dig in the flower garden, do the work around there, and she'd always let me say what we were going to have for lunch or dinner. She said I was "the man of the house" when her husband wasn't there or before he gets off. He'd come when I got off in the evening. I'd work until around 5:00. That's the usual time back then. I would already have said what we were going to have, what we were going to have for lunch and for dinner. And she taught us to eat some meals we hadn't had before. We ate practically everything we could get. The cook—my sister used to be the cook—she would . . . I know you haven't ever seen any of this—take the leftover bread, cornbread, and fix it like you fix dressing, put onions and stuff in the bread, and put it in the stove and brown it. Wouldn't be no chicken or anything in it. Sometimes she would just make it in a frying pan. Baking and all that takes time. Would be something they called coosh.

When the soldiers come back, they come back. I just remember when my brother-in-law come.

LESTER: And this was 1919?

HENDERSON: And he went to France and back. When he come back, the white people treated colored people kind of bad. They didn't want you to wear the uniform when you come back. Some didn't have nothing else to wear. Some of them Ku Klux, they didn't have on their robes and things at the time, but they would cut the buttons off. A group of them would get together and cut the buttons off your uniform, your army uniform. And "nigger"—I resent that now. I guess I'll resent that [name] all of my life.

LESTER: And that was a common word then?

HENDERSON: Common word white folks used, that word "nigger." Some of them still do. I started going to the gym. We had a little gym on 27th Street and Avenue C, 3rd Avenue and 27th Street. Go down there and work out and train, training for boxing. When I was about 17 or 18 or 19 or 20, something like that. The white man called me a nigger, I'd make him take it back. I'd beat him to death, beat him much as you can and then run, run somewhere and hide. Sometimes you wish you hadn't done it because you'd be so scared. (Laughs)

LESTER: So what was education like? You said you would caddy at the country club and then come back and go to school.

HENDERSON: Yeah, well see I'd be up that morning at 5:00, maybe out there with whoever it be. Mr. W. W. French was what we called a "good man."

LESTER: So he was a good white man?

HENDERSON: Yes sir. He was a good white man. He would be up there, and his brother, and then late in the afternoon after school was out he would be up there, he and his brother, and then late in the afternoon after school was out, I would go back to the club. I would run from

Thomas School up to the club. Usually I'd caddy for Mr. Stockard, the man that owned the Stockard Pipe Place. I'd caddy for him. He had a son, Hubbard. Hubbard, he didn't like black people.

LESTER: Were your other brothers caddying too, or was this only you? Your sisters were usually cooking or housekeeping?

HENDERSON: And if they wasn't doing that, they was working for some white people somewhere.

LESTER: Is that the kind of work they'd be doing? Cleaning houses or keeping kids?

HENDERSON: Yeah. Cleaning houses, keeping the children, cooking, doing everything. My sister was waiting for Mrs. Newton. I think a lot of Mrs. Newton, fine woman, good white lady. Her husband was a good white man, as far as I was concerned. She was a friend, you know. "Bottom rail come on top." She wanted to have some friends, she said that.

LESTER: Tell me that saying again.

HENDERSON: "The bottom rail gonna come to the top," the scripture says. It say that in the scripture. But, what the black people wanted it to mean was "One of these days they were gonna be above the white man." And some of the white people, they feared that. You know your real friends don't care how high or how low. The old people would sometimes say that.

LESTER: Right.

HENDERSON: Sometimes at old dry goods store where you would go. 47th Street and 6th Avenue and head on over 28th Street and 7th Avenue over on 27th Street was one that most of the black people went to. And if you go down there to the dry store, white boys were always hanging out down there. I would be kinda scared to go through to the dry store, but you had to go if your parents sent you. When I went, I always had bricks in my pockets. Carried bricks in my hip pockets when I go down there, carried them in my side pocket. If anybody hit me, I was gonna hit 'em back. That's what you were taught back then. See black people were taught right. You were probably taught if anybody hit you, hit 'em back. They do in your time. Well, it was worse back then. If anybody hit me, I hit 'em back. I hit you back with my hand.

LESTER: And that wasn't more dangerous 'cause if you hit another white person, wouldn't you be . . .

HENDERSON: Running scared. You'd be running scared.

LESTER: But you'd be scared anyway.

HENDERSON: Yeah, you'd be scared anyway.

LESTER: Did that mean that black people just stayed in all the time or off the streets at certain times?

HENDERSON: When the Ku Klux said, that's the only time they'd be off.

LESTER: All other times they'd be just like they are now?

HENDERSON: Going anywhere they wanted to go.

LESTER: They just knew to stay in their place?

HENDERSON: Yeah, because you'd have a place, but you see I didn't have a place. I associated with the rich white folk.

LESTER: Right.

HENDERSON: I was a caddy. My thing was to carry the bag, tell that [white] man my best idea about what club to use. If he liked that, maybe I'd get a nickel more, maybe a dime.

LESTER: Then I guess it was good to know a rich or influential white person in case you were in a tight spot and needed help?

HENDERSON: That's right. You really needed a good white person in 1931. I believe it was 1931 or 1932, the year the banks closed.

LESTER: The Great Depression.

HENDERSON: Right, the fact that the banks closed wasn't no concern of mine [as a black person], no poor white folks for that matter. (Laughs)

LESTER: (Laughing) Right.

HENDERSON: It was cold and had rained and it froze. It snowed a little, rained a little and iced over. You could slip on the ground. Terrible time to work. That was either 1931 or 1932. So, we didn't have no coal and nothing to eat in the house. We didn't have nothing to make a meal, but I knowed a [white] man. I used to sell him golf balls. My mind fell on him, and I was going to ask him for help. So I called him. I don't remember but one black family having a telephone between 29th and 30th Street. There in the alley, a black lady had a phone. Her husband worked for some white people and they had him a phone put in so they could keep close contact with him. When they wanted him and they wanted to use him (laughs), they supposed they could call him. Well everybody wanted to call somebody, but you didn't have anybody to call. (Laughs) So they would go up to this lady's house. His name was John. He chauffeured. I don't know where he learned to drive a car. But if you learned how to drive a car, you'll get a job working as a chauffeur. Now, you'd do everything. You'd wash the dishes, mow the lawn. You'd do everything. But you was the chauffeur, when the lady—most likely the man would be gone to work—would say, "Alright, in now and get dressed, I want you to drive me." I went down there and called this man named Mr. Brushevski. I know where he lives at right now. I know he ain't hardly moved cause his home right over there. And I said, "Mr. Brushevski, this is Joe," and he said, "Joe, yeah, I know who you are." I tell that the weather was bad and when the weather is bad you can't caddy in the ice and the snow. The ball go under the snow. You can't find the ball. It ain't time for golf. Food was out, the coal was out, and the house wasn't the best house to be in when you had a fire. So I said, "I want to borrow some money from you til the weather change." He said, "Joe, don't you know that the banks closed?" I said, "Yes, sir." He said, "I ain't got no money." I said, "Mr. Brushevski, you ain't got all your money in the bank and the bank done closed." I said, "You know the bank was gonna close before they closed." Well, I know what I was telling him was that he was a white man. And he knowed what was going on too. You know we knowed. First time I ever saw one of those things you pulled out—a stopwatch—was at his house. So I told him that my daddy was always never scared of nobody, don't care what color he was. Pap wasn't scared. He said, "I ain't got no money." I said, "Ah, Mr. Brushevski, let me have some money. I need some money." He said, "I ain't got none," and he went and hung up. I said, "I know Mr. Brushevski got money."

I got out and went right down to 5th Avenue. I went down there and went in his [Mr. Brushevski's] office, and one of the other fellows—he knew me too because I went in there all the time—said, "Sit down, Joe." I sit down and heard him tell Mr. Brushevski, "Joe out here." He said, "I know he out there." I didn't like the tone he said it in, but I wasn't fixin' to go nowhere, and I didn't. So I stayed on to closing time. So he said, "Joe, didn't I tell you I didn't have no money?" I said, "Yes sir, you told me that." I said, "But I thought you probably had 'enough' money, and I ain't got no coal at my house, and I'm the seventh in my family. There's six older than me. All of us there at the house except my oldest brother, next oldest brother." They might not have been there. My sisters, all them there. He said, "Well, come in here." So I went on in there, sat down. I sat on that side of the desk, and he sat in his regular chair. He said, "What'd you have in mind, Joe? How was you gonna do if I wasn't gonna let you have nothing?" I said, "I don't know sir what I was going to do. I wasn't gonna do anything." What I was saying was there wasn't nothing for me to do except ask someone else who I thought might lend me the money. So he said, "Alright, are you gonna pay me back?" I said, "Yes sir, I'm gonna pay you back." I wasn't trying to borrow a whole lot—five or ten dollars. I doubted who would steal it. Anyway, he let me have it. He said, "I want to tell you something: from this day on if you have some important things—your coal is out and groceries out—don't call a man. Go to him and tell him your troubles, and he might do like I did." I said, "Well, yes sir, from now on I'll do that. I hope there's not gonna be another time, but I expect there will be another time." That was when you've gotta act now. It was dead winter time, snow and ice out there and you ain't got nothing to eat. You got to do something. You've got to talk to some people or see if they'll do something. If they don't, well you know you tried.

LESTER: Right.

HENDERSON: So he let me have the money. So we were kinda friendly then. When he said I had to pay him back, I had to caddy for him, go to his house, cut the lawn, had to do everything to pay him back.

LESTER: I see.

HENDERSON: I was thankful, you know how thankful I was. I guess I was 22 years old in 1932. I paid him back and he never did call me a "nigger." The rich people always called me by my name, Joe. Them poor ones, I'd make them regret it. (Laughs) That's like I'd have somebody run and hide. Ain't nowhere to run. Run to your house, over to my house, over to your house so you'd knock one of those white boys in the head or something. There'd be like five or six of them jump on you. You didn't have no choice. You'd be kicking, doing anything. Well, two things nobody do to me: call me a "nigger" and kick me. If you kick me, something was going to happen to you. I had my weapons in my pocket. I got Mr. Brushevski's money paid back and everything. He thought very highly of me. And I would go there and eat.

LESTER: Yes.

HENDERSON: A meal was something then. I would go to his house in the evening time. "Joe come by there and cut the grass." "Yes Sir." I would go by there, cut the grass, and they would pay me what little they did, and give me a meal. That would be one less meal that would have to be eat at home.

LESTER: At home, right.

HENDERSON: A little more for the rest of them, that's exactly right.

LESTER: So were the white people worse on the boys than they were on the girls, or were they equally rough and threatening?

HENDERSON: No, they didn't hardly bother the girls, very seldom. One might try to get smart with one once in a while. They didn't see the girls where they hang out. But they wouldn't bother girls none, maybe try to get smart with them. But girls wouldn't pay them no attention.

LESTER: But the boys though, like the time you told me about the man being castrated. When was that?

HENDERSON: I don't know what year that was.

LESTER: Were you a young boy then?

HENDERSON: I was plenty old enough to remember. I don't remember what year, but I remember real well.

LESTER: And that was here in Birmingham?

HENDERSON: Yeah, I don't remember exactly where. What I heard was it was over by Stucker in 1911 or 1912. They were woods people. It wasn't built up like it is now, and I don't know whether this is the truth. They wanted to—that sounds so bad—wanted a governor or mayor, and certain things happen in Alabama that the mayor don't like. And the governor wanted a big state and this is a pretty nice place to live, blacks and whites. That's what they want. But what I was talking about was a setup. A white man was going to join the KKK. You have to do something to show that you're a member of the KKK, just some load of nonsense.

LESTER: Initiation?

HENDERSON: Yeah, so this fellow was cutting up [acting like a fool] somewhere, over there somewhere. They caught him, picked him up, throwed him in the car, carried him somewhere. I don't know if they did it right there or what. Where it was it was still over there and they carried him somewhere and castrated him and put some salt like they do a hog. You ever see 'em cut a hog? Well, when they cut a hog like that, well, they cut him and they take out what you can call "mountain oyster." They take them out and you eat them, and they did him just like that. They put all that, some say it was kerosene, some say it was turpentine. I don't know what it was, and salt, and they put that down between his legs. The doctor say if they hadn't have put that down between his legs, he would have died, bled to death. And this white fellow joined the KKK and see what happened? Some of the higher ups wanted to know why did they do this, and this reporter went to go see what happened and they told him. I remember reading something in the newspaper. I was going to school at the time, but I don't remember how it read. He was just messed up. You know the difference between a steer and a bull?

LESTER: Yes.

HENDERSON: Well, he was just like a steer.

LESTER: And nothing was done about it?

HENDERSON: No, wasn't nothing done about it. Nothing hardly that a white man couldn't do to black man. If you and a white man get into it out in the street, get to fighting, you wasn't gonna bother the white man. The white man would mess with you, but you know better than to bother the white man. When the police or some other white folks see y'all out there fighting or having words or anything, they'd call the police. Well, the police come carry you to jail and leave the white man there.

LESTER: No matter what was happening?

HENDERSON: No matter what was happening.

LESTER: You were already guilty?

HENDERSON: That's right.

LESTER: Did any of your family go up north during all of this? There were a lot of people going to the North, leaving the South because of all this kind of unjust treatment.

HENDERSON: Well, no, my family, sisters and brothers, they didn't go as the people say, "up north." They go east or west, though they say north. They didn't go anyplace. My sisters, they went away from here, just not long before the war. The war started in 1941. Everybody remembers that day, December 7, 1941. That's the day I'll remember as long as I live. They went. One of my sisters went. Then later, another sister went. They were the first ones to leave. The only time I've lived away from Birmingham was when I was in the army.

LESTER: And did things seem to change when you were in the army? I know it was a different time then. Were race relations better then, worse, or about the same?

HENDERSON: We were stationed down in Florida when the word come from President Roosevelt. That was close to 1942. I went in the army in 1942, in July. Well shortly—I don't know how long we'd been there; I don't know whether the year had been out or not, 1942 or 1943. They said the President, the Commander-in-Chief, said, "No more segregation on the army field, busing, nowhere." They had something they called the PX, and they had one, kinda a nice place. You know how they fix them for the white folks. (Laughs)

Well at that time, I was MP [Military Police] in the army. I didn't want the job, but you do what they tell you to do. So I told the Court Board Marshal, which is the law in the army, and went over and told that I didn't want to be an MP, and he asked me why I didn't want to be an MP. And black folks looked upon police as they were always somebody to throw you in jail and beat you. There was no one to protect you. Now, I didn't think that was going to do that, but I just didn't want to be a police 'cause that's all I had ever known. So he said—they all called me "Hennison." He said, "Hennison, the reason you don't want to be an MP is 'cause you got too many friends and you don't want to come in contact with none of your friends." I said, "What you mean? What you mean, come in contact with?" I said, "All the police I see beat up black folks." And I was mostly going to be where black folks was until this happened and until the President said, "No more segregation on army fields."

We had a good commanding officer. He was an officer out of World

War I, Major Nielsen. I am always fortunate one way or the other. The
fellows went up to what they call the PX, white folks' PX. Word was there
wasn't no more of that—black on one side and white on the other. It
wasn't supposed to be so and President Roosevelt was in Washington.

LESTER: And he couldn't have any idea that was common where you
lived?

HENDERSON: Right.

LESTER: And people respected that. What other kinds of things were segregated? Water fountains? Bathrooms? Washing rooms? Hospitals?

HENDERSON: Oh yes, water fountains. Yeah, they always did segregate
you if you went to the hospital. Down in both sides, black people was
doing now like the young people do. They be hurting one another. They
wouldn't be hurting the white folks. I be wondering all the time, "If you
was going to kill somebody, why don't you kill some of the white people
that be messing with you instead of black folks?" I know that if I was
going to kill, that's who I'd kill. So he said that and the fellows he was
their commanding officer, he said, "I know that what's been said by the
President, and I know what you supposed to do." "But see," he said.
Now this was just down these fellows' alley. When they found out, they
went up to the white people's place.

The Marshall says, "Where are they?" I always keep my reservations
about things, and I was uptight. And he said, "If there is any way he
could, he would." I reckon he never talked to him or told him there
wasn't no way to get any word but it wasn't 'bout twenty minutes they
could have walked the woods. But as God would have it, they didn't get
any word. And the Marshall sat up there and told them to come back
down there where they belonged. And they wouldn't come. Then they
got some more MP's and some hickory sticks and come there and told
them to leave. They didn't want to leave. They said, "Get in a formation
and go back down there where you was." Says "it's just plain stupid for
y'all to come up here and start this up and call the commanding officer."
I wouldn't go up there. Well, he was right. In a way, he was right. I know
what the law says. But has it ever mattered to the white folks what the
law says?

LESTER: Right, historically.

HENDERSON: I'm talkin 'bout it wouldn't be nothing. The law downtown, what the Man [white people] was saying. He was downtown, and
we was all up and down the Southside and everywhere else. The best
thing to do, you didn't want to run and hide. See if you run and hide
for one day, it wouldn't do you no good. You have to stay here for a
while. But very seldom you found that kind. But Mr. Doc said, "Alright,
you done told us so run along." And he didn't leave it alone. He pulled

up one of the poles. Those posts were nailed up, and he went and ripped out one by one four of them and like to beat that white man to death. You see you just find one person like that every once in a while. And Mr. Doc beat him down to the ground. And he had this nice hat, and said, "That's alright, that's alright, just be here tonight." He said, "I'm coming back and you know what that means." It means the Ku Klux coming. Mr. Doc was a man I think all folks look alike to him. And if you done the wrong thing . . . He run that white man out of town. But didn't nobody come back that night. I was scared all night. I thought the Ku Klux was gonna come. They was gonna do a lot. But didn't no one come that night, not a single soul. Well, well, Mr. Doc didn't go nowhere, and I didn't see the pistol, but they say he had a pistol down there, go anywhere he want to go and nobody better not bother him. That's Mr. Doc. But wasn't but one Mr. Doc Brown.

LESTER: (Laughs) Mr. Doc couldn't protect everybody.

HENDERSON: No, he couldn't protect himself, but he didn't come. He wasn't going to bother them, but they best not bother him. That's the way he was.

LESTER: Now when did you and your wife marry? Was that after you got out of the army, or while you were in the army?

HENDERSON: It was before I got in. I went down to go in and I came home on furlough. Well, you not a soldier until you headed off for war. So I come back and I was sworn in, ten or fifteen days. Well, when I come back from down there, I married. The reason I went and married, she wouldn't have nothing to live on. Time was still hard in the 1940s. It was hard for some people in the 1940s as it was back in the 1930s. So my sister-in-law, well, her brother's sister said, "You need to try to fix up some kind of way so that Louise can have something to live on." I don't know what I said to that right there; it wasn't nothing about I'm gonna marry her. I underline everything folks say to me. I want to see my thoughts and what yours are. So I said, "Well, I don't know." So I thought about it. She didn't have nothing to live on. She was living off the job that I worked. So it occurred to me that it would be a good idea if I did marry so that she could get along. So we went to the courthouse and married. When I went back down there, I had a wife and learned down there that the army will honor a common law wife. He said, "You have a wife?" He knew I wasn't married. "Did you used to stay with a woman?" And I said, "Yeah. I stayed with one before I came here." I went on and straightened that out. Then when I went down there, I got sworn in.

LESTER: Did your brother go into service too?

HENDERSON: My brother that you know [Thomas Henderson] went into service back in 1940. Let me see here, 1939 or 1940. You was enlisted in the army for a year and then you came back home. Well, I say, it's because if a war was to break out, then the soldiers would already be trained. Well, my brother went, then my brother Tom, my older brother. I had been in, I guess 1943, when he got in. I got a brother named John; he got in the army then. A hundred and thirteen of us was in when I went overseas. I went to Hawaii first, then to Japan. From Japan and then to Okinawa. Okinawa, they say, is 350 miles from Japan. Well, during the time I was there, at one time during World War II, they had over one million men there and we was there. That was 1945. Must have been around the first of 1945 'cause they was bombing Japan and the last resistance Japan had. United States caught the planes on the ground and bombed them on the ground. They didn't even get airborne, and we would ask the pilot, "How did it look over there?" He would answer, "I didn't see nothing but fires everywhere." Well, when the Japanese didn't have any resistance except for a few scattered around, a few diehards, I said, "Man, how long is this thing going to be?" He said, "It can't be too long." He didn't look to go back no more. Something like that with all good talk, which is what we wanted to hear. They couldn't, didn't have anything to fight with. They quit bombings; they just light fires with an incinerator. Now, incinerators don't go out. You throw it in the water and it don't go out. Burn until it goes out. That's what they was doing. Dropping it on Japan, lighting fires. Well, the Japanese had tunnels underground that run from one to another. If you run in one here, and they had flame throwers, the United States had flame throwers, and you put them in the holes. Some didn't come out then. They'd die right there, burn till it killed them. If they run in there, you think they right there, but they could be a mile across town. During that time, everybody considered, we did, we knew it wasn't but a matter of time. What we were told was, they went to Washington to try to negotiate some kind of deal with the U.S. government. What it was, was hard to do I imagine. See they bombed Pearl Harbor and the conclusion they told us what they want you to know. They had said before, right at that time, right before then. This guy, the name I can't recall, say, "The American soldiers better give up." I don't know how long, but he was gonna whup [beat] America and he gonna be at the White House dictating what to say. Well, we all have our opinions, and I didn't believe that. I said he could, or it might be true according to what's said and who says it. In the next two or three days, they said Japan had surrendered. Well, we went last but we come back some of the first. I went over to Japan looking for my brother, but they told me, "Well, you know you can always find where that is. You go back over to the States." He had been in about a year when they bombed Pearl Harbor.

LESTER: Well, tell me about what black folks did when the white people weren't around and always threatening.

HENDERSON: What would they do?

LESTER: Yeah, I mean, what would they do when they were together? What would they talk about? What kinds of things would the black people do when the whites weren't around?

HENDERSON: The ones who weren't scared to talk.

LESTER: We hear a lot about people sitting on porches, and I know church was a big part of black life as well.

HENDERSON: That [church] was the thing.

LESTER: Was that the central social point right then? So religion was extremely important?

HENDERSON: That was the social circle. You know when you get scared, you gonna pray.

LESTER: And you were always scared?

HENDERSON: Black people was scared of white people, but my daddy never told us to be afraid. Never told me or any of my brothers to be afraid. He said, "Don't get into it with white people. But if you get into it with them, do anything you can to them because they gonna kill you. Whatever you can—kill them—whatever you could do 'cause they was gonna kill you."

LESTER: Now was that the lesson you also got from church? What kinds of mixed messages were you getting? Was race always an element as part of the service?

HENDERSON: No.

LESTER: Were you always talking about white people?

HENDERSON: No, sometimes . . . some black persons, most likely a man, the KKK done burnt your house down, done beat you or something, maybe they killed you, and then some people would be afraid to talk about it in the church. Wasn't nothing but blacks in the church. Shoot, you know some blacks talk to whites. They tell white folks what they wasn't telling you. They talked more 'bout whites and blacks during integration, during Martin Luther King's time more than I ever heard mention, but they were afraid too, a lot of people. When you go to church, you kinda want to hear a sermon. You want to hear something uplifting. But if something go down, they publish it in the newspapers. You get you a *Birmingham News* or *Birmingham Herald*, you look at it and see what done happened. Nothing done about it. "It'll teach y'all niggers a lesson." If you done something, they do something low down, beat you to death, burn your house down.

LESTER: Did you know anyone personally that had that happen to them, had their houses burned or somebody who was killed? Or were they just people that the community knew about?

HENDERSON: No, I didn't know anybody like I know somebody in the neighborhood. And they killed somebody. Usually the Ku Klux take you out of the neighborhood. There was plenty of woods, take you to the woods. Well on the Southside on 28th Street there was a field up there where John Carter had fields planted right in front of Grant Chapel, fields planted with corn and cotton. People would hunt, go catch rabbits. Grant Chapel wasn't up there. The minister then was Reverend Tyler and the church moved, and we went to church every Sunday. You have some always that will do what they want. People said that you can't just tell your children to go to church, you got to carry them. Well, don't no one carry me. They told us, "Get up, get ready, and go to Sunday school." But at our church, I guess you heard, the Christian Devil lived? The Baptists had BYBU [white Baptist Youth Bible Union]. That church been down there a long time. All the good boys go down there, where all the girls go. They say the morning you leave, "Don't go down to 32nd this evening. Stay up there at Grant Chapel where you belong." Well, children feared parents then. I was looking at the TV the other day, there's this gang out at Chicago that killed a girl. And a boy 13 or 14 years old, and one of them boys was 10 but he belonged to the gang. He threatened his father, all that kind of stuff like that going on. I said, "My God, I wonder what I would have done [if that was my child]?" I don't know. My children don't talk back to me. My papa, well you knew you weren't gonna talk back to him, and you better not talk back to mama.

LESTER: You said that your dad was never afraid of anybody and told you never to bow your heads. What did your mother say, or did she say anything about how to survive?

HENDERSON: No. I don't remember her saying. Only thing I remember her saying was, "If anybody hit you, hit them back." They was talking about that in Sunday School. Say you're supposed to turn cheek, but she said that started wrong. You know some people didn't understand what they read. Can't go by what somebody else say. All I ever thought was that; that was my code. If you hit me, I hit you back, and then when I went into the prize ring, I hear my manager from the side of the ring yelling, "Hit him! Hit him! Hit him back! He hit you harder than you hit him!"

LESTER: You were a boxer?

HENDERSON: Yeah.

LESTER: When were you a boxer?

HENDERSON: I don't know how many years. We had a group. We'd go from one side of town to the other in search of a match. We'd come to Avondale [a section of Birmingham] at a certain time, and then managers would come to our place and bring their fighters and we'd fight there and then just all around. You fight all the time. The only thing you could fight was a curtain riser. A curtain riser is something before the main bout, before the white folks. We got paid too. They'd give you a dollar a round. And you know a dollar ain't nothing, but it was something then. And people would throw money up into the ring. Sometimes those people would throw a dollar. And everywhere I was fighting didn't nobody go with you. It would be four or five other fighters from down around there. That's who would be there and all the grown-ups would be trainers. There weren't a lot of black folks coming down there to watch you fight.

LESTER: Who trained you then?

HENDERSON: I was trained by Clarence LaRay. "The Warmest Terror" was his fighting name. I guess he was good enough, but I guess he wasn't as good as I always thought he was. But he would fight anybody. Well, all of us fought any weight. That's like I wanted to weigh round 180 to 185 pounds when I wanted to beat some big guy. Then I would get back down to 159 or 160 back and forth, according to who I was going to fight.

LESTER: How long were you a boxer? Just while you were a teenager?

HENDERSON: Yeah, I was from age 15. I started working in the mine with my father at age 17. I wasn't but 17 in 1927. Well, you had the arena down there. We didn't get nothing for fighting, nothing when you went to the auditorium. Well, we used to fight right there at 32nd Street and 6th Avenue. It was a big open field all the way up to Clairmont Avenue. We played golf, football, baseball, and had fights. Most of the fights could have benefited the whites on Sunday. Well, we had, I guess, a hole dug in the ground and white people would come out there and throw pennies, nickels, dimes, and quarters. Some of the rich ones would throw a 50-cent piece or a dollar.

LESTER: Did that go to both of you or to the winner?

HENDERSON: That went to both people.

LESTER: So nobody really got hurt?

HENDERSON: Nobody got no bones broken.

LESTER: You might get bruised?

HENDERSON: Well, you gonna get knocked down.

LESTER: Right, but it wasn't trying to get blood? This was a community, social thing.

HENDERSON: Well, some people's nose is easy to bleed and the mouth and around the eyes. I had a good friend who said, "Hit people and don't let them hit you back. If you go into a fighter, you hit and then you get back outside, or you go into him so that his arm or his fists couldn't hit you, so that it go around you." That's what they teach you. If you stand there, you might get killed. That's the way we used to be fighting, and right there, right off of Green Spring Avenue [Southside Birmingham]—that barbeque place is over there now—they had a big ring. They'd have big fights there. They'd give you a little something. Well, they'd usually give the fighters some money. That wouldn't be all the time. Not all of them would be that at the same time, and when we was going to fight somewhere some wouldn't want to go. Just want to go. Some go just to look, some not go at all.

First of all, you walked everywhere you went. You didn't have no car to ride in, not back then. Everywhere you go, you walked. I used to go to Stoken. They kinda good baseball team. What they called the Red Diamond, where that park is, baseball diamond. "Well, are you going to the ball game?" "Yeah, I'm going." You come right down 32nd Street to railroad tracks, then you go across something called a coal pile, then cross by Thomas School. That's where I went to school at. Go right by that school, get through there, to city league. They played some ball games to you now.

LESTER: As far as schooling, did they have grades that you go through? How far did you go?

HENDERSON: Yeah, you finish grade school. When you finish eighth grade, you go to high school.

LESTER: Now, high school, was that until the twelfth grade?

HENDERSON: Yeah, til twelfth grade. Now, that was a way long time ago. It was industrial. I guess you heard of that?

LESTER: Tell me about the music during the 1920s and 1930s. Do you remember anything about the music in particular?

HENDERSON: The music in the 1930s was people, mostly singers, who had entertaining songs, but the blues was the main thing, W. C. Handy with his "St. Louis Blues." Now, people sang all kinds of blues. I will never forget when my brother came out of the army, they was singing some kind of blues I done forgot now—sugar blues, everybody's favorite sugar blues. And then, after that as I grew up they had a show downtown Birmingham, the Frolic Theater. They would have an act or two a night. Whatever you know how to do, then you could win the contest. You might win ten or fifteen dollars, big money. You would have so much for dancing, so much for singing. Well, the women would sing the blues back then; they didn't sing like the men from your time. They sang the blues. Well, Bessie Smith, Mamie Smith, Ida Cox, she was a great. She played in movies. And Ma Rainey could "holler like a mountain jack/she could get way up on the mountain and call her babies back." (Laughs) Then later Bessie Smith and Mamie Smith, Ida Cox, and Ma Rainey were the main singers, and they could do it.

LESTER: And what were they singing about? What was the blues? Was it just the rhythm of it that had a kind of church sound to it?

HENDERSON: It was what it was. You know what the blues is, don't you?

LESTER: You tell me what it is.

HENDERSON: The blues is a woman wanting to see her man, or vice versa. That's what they be singing about. That's the blues.

LESTER: And there was kind of a church connection to the blues, wasn't there? Not literally.

HENDERSON: I understand what you saying. It's just like it is now. Good singers in the church could get more money singing the blues, or singing the songs that they sing now than you can singing in church. See you might not get paid nothing in the church way back then.

LESTER: But that was a good training ground.

HENDERSON: Yeah, it was a good training ground to learn how to sing.

LESTER: You can still hear some of those blues rhythms in some of those gospel songs.

HENDERSON: I sit here and look at a man on the TV [commercial], and he was singing "Ain't got no shirt. Ain't got no shoes. Ain't got no coat. Better get me the blues." His wife says it was the worship. You ain't got no Pepsi, that's all that's wrong with you. You know he be on there sometimes. All them women coming singing the blues and the men start dancing and they sing and dance. They have all kinds of different things, you know—have a big time down there. If you want to, anybody could compete down there.

LESTER: And no white people around then?

HENDERSON: The white people didn't bar you from the Frolic, but there would be some there sometimes to see the show.

LESTER: But not trying to control the show?

HENDERSON: No, no.

LESTER: Just like the church, that was safety.

HENDERSON: Yeah, they [whites] come and listen to the songs. I went to hear the blues but also to see the dance and to crack jokes, to see the women 'cause you would see some with shorts on. All of them comedians who come from here went up north. And all them up north they tour, come over here and down through there. Anywhere. They would have some real good shows. I danced, I mean buck-danced. People wanted to see you dance. My brother, both of them, the dude was the poorest dancer. He could dance a little, but not like the rest of us. I watched my older brother dance, and he said, "See, you can do this." My knees are bad now or I could demonstrate. On the floor, you need the sound; sound is the tap dancer. Everybody knew who was the best dancer. Everybody called him Bye Joe. His name was Eddie Williams. He could dance. And we would have contests, and I would say, "Have you seen this step before, and can you cut this step?" Sometimes there might be two or three of us. Everybody knew who was the best. Some people liked some people better than others. I was doing it for dance. I wasn't trying to make a living. I'm a golf player, prize-fighter and golf player.

LESTER: When would they go to the Frolic, on Friday nights?

HENDERSON: Oh no, on Mondays. We go to three shows. Friday night, we go to 18th Street. Right on Fourth Avenue was the Frolic. That's where you have the vaudeville shows. We had some real good vaudeville shows. Some great singers. All them people used to come hear all those great singers I mentioned. And the men when they started singing, the men did the most dancing and cracking jokes. And they didn't always sing the blues; they sang other songs.

LESTER: Tell me about the cracking jokes. What kind of cracking jokes would the men do?

HENDERSON: They cracked jokes about each other, or what have you. This old man asked "Ha, Ha, have you seen the wind blow?" And the fellow said, "I seen the wind blow so hard it blowed down trees and chopped off houses." He said, "You talking about a whirlwind." (Laughs) You know what a whirlwind is? So he said, "What you talking about? Man, I seen the wind blow so hard it blowed a wash pot inside out. It blowed the time back two, three hours and turned the moon around." (Laughs). All kinds of jokes, it was very entertaining. The biggest entertainment black folks had back then was the Frolic Theater. We had a show at the Masonic Temple, right there on 17th. This was some social club that was way on down. The social club, they asked the people to come to the major show. I danced, some sang, and some of the girls sang. It was pretty good size then. I thought I was in school then. A girl, she would sing "All in Love." And at the end of the school year, you would have a concert and you do what you can do, or are willing to do. And each class competed against each other then. So you teach two fifth grade classes, two or all of them. Didn't have no two eighth grade classes. Eighth grade, you were getting ready for high school. The school I went to over there.

LESTER: Is that Thomas or Thompson?

HENDERSON: Thomas. Well at that school, the principal was W. C. Davis. He was a little man. I guess he weighted no more than 150 something, but he was a gritty little man. Well, large children went to school and some big old mean ones, and you'd think they would just mash him up one day, but they never did. He'd tell them he had them in control. My hat's off to him for a guy that size grabbing them over in the corner weighing about 200. So I said, "Don't do it." So he said, "If you do it, I don't know what I do to you, just shake it." W. C. Davis was a man. He was a man. They had some teachers too. I never will forget when I went to third grade. During an examination I made a hundred in every subject to get promoted. And they carried me around and showed me to the classes of the school, and said, "Here is a boy—some of you hope to get promoted, think you'll get promoted—well he knows he'll get promoted." I didn't say anything, I didn't even say I had made a hundred. A teacher by the name of Whitman, she said it.

LESTER: Remember much about the Civil Rights movement?

HENDERSON: I had been a prize fighter coming up. I didn't march with the marches 'cause I had been taught to hit back. Like when you are driving a car, and you see another car, you don't need to look for the brake, you know where the brake is. Well, when you train to fight, you train to be a soldier and you do what you been trained to do. If anybody hit me, I hit back. They didn't want anybody that would hit back. That was completely out. Don't hit back and if they asked you what would you do if this happened to you, you might say, "Well, I guess I'd hit back. What would you do?" I was taught at home if anybody hit me, hit them back. That mostly applied to black children. But when I went to the prize ring, they was still telling me the same thing. Back in the services they would tell you how much courage to display. They'd send you down through the jungle and you'd have certain things protecting you, but you wouldn't know it until you had been down there and got your jungle training. Well, when I went down and got my jungle training, I was used to fighting back, always fighting back, fighting back, fight, fight, fighting back. If anybody do something to you, get them back.

LESTER: So King came talking all that, and that . . .

HENDERSON: That was the wrong way; it was the wrong way and it was right. First place, the black people didn't have a chance to whup [beat] the white people. There's more of them than you. And they had been trained and you ain't, all this kind of stuff. When they really started to fear you was when you came out of that army; they knew you had some training then. White folks didn't want to fool with black folks. But if there's five of them and one of you, well and good; they kick you all over the place.

LESTER: Did you know anything about Malcolm X? What was your attitude toward what he was saying?

HENDERSON: Malcolm X said the white people brought our foreparents here and made them slaves. He said they owed us. And I said, "They work us and it's definitely certain they owe us." He said a lot of things like that. He would be talking and then he got this idea of the white folks paying us for our forefathers' working in slavery. That's when they took him out, and some of them think that the white folks did kill him. The black folks did it, but I say the white folks really killed him. Black folks killed him, but the white folks paid them to kill him. Malcolm X was my hero. He was going around and he was talking, going everywhere talking. He wasn't scared. If you say that Dr. Martin Luther King wasn't scared of anybody, you could see that he [King] wasn't scared of anybody. If he was, he wouldn't be around here. Well, Malcolm X was the same way. He wasn't scared of anybody. He would go anywhere; he didn't care what white folks think.

I went to church and heard Thurgood Marshall, and he later became Supreme Court Justice. Before he became that, he had a high position I can't remember. I said, "I am going to go down here and hear what Thurgood Marshall has to say." And I went down there, downtown, and we went in there. It was a pretty big church, but the church wasn't full. It had two or three police in there. "In this church here," he had a deep voice you know. "In this church here, it ought to be full, it shouldn't be standing room, but the people are scared of Bull Connor. That's all he is, just bull, but he got y'all [blacks] scattered." Some people ain't scared of nobody, don't care who you are or where you live. They don't care. And after that night, I said, "Thurgood Marshall ain't scared of nobody and he was Attorney General."

LESTER: He was pretty loud while he was a Justice, too.

HENDERSON: He got a big voice.

LESTER: He is a big man.

HENDERSON: He was a big man. You could hear it when he spoke. I look at my heroes, like him and I think, "That man right there, somebody might kill him at any time, like Martin Luther King." But what actually happened to Martin Luther King when everybody was talking about somebody gonna kill him, ain't nothing happened. In my opinion, he had God with him to a point. All of Christ's disciples, Moses, all of the people of the Bible died, and that means you got to. And them people they knowed it and that they had to go, but they had to say it. They knew the danger there was. They let you leave with a little more courage than when you went there, and they said what would you look like if you let a white man hit you, kick you around in the street, and you not hit back. You see some black people they would do that. Some black people, they wouldn't hit back, but you better not hit me. I don't care what color you are.

LESTER: You're one feisty man.

HENDERSON: I guess it's just the way you feel, and what you talk. You know you ain't got a chance if you get into it, so you might as well help yourself. I always had a knife I carried all the time. I quit carrying it a few years ago. I carry a pistol. I had a killer knife. The saying is, "Plant that knife in the left shirt pocket, close to your heart. If you do that you won't hardly have no trouble with that person, not there, if they made it." You know, I thought I could protect myself.

LESTER: You weren't out starting stuff?

HENDERSON: No, didn't bother nobody. Didn't start nothing, but nobody better bother me. I never will forget the one morning—I guess about two or three o'clock in the morning. A lot of stealing had been done on the Southside, from 33rd Street clean down. Some people I forgot to tell you about, and I don't know last name. He was working for an ice cream company, good ice cream. He wanted a raise, but the white folks wouldn't give him no raise. He had worries concerning his money. He put him up a little place. You know how we put up a little place. The city inspector came down there every Monday and poured the ice cream out and said it wasn't sanitary. And he come down there like this Monday and poured his ice cream out and said, "You better never come down here no more and pour my ice cream out 'cause it is sanitary. All my things are clean. It's as clean as the place I used to work at. I know that's how come you doing that." He wasn't afraid of nobody; he talked that. And the police come down there next Monday—he had ice cream in those five-gallon things—and poured it right off the curbstone. And his blood was running right down that gutter with that ice cream. He killed him. He shot him and killed him. And two police come right quick and he took them out afterward. That was down on 18th Street.

LESTER: And when was that?

HENDERSON: I don't know what year that was. I might could find someone that might know. Let me call Jessie Blackmon [another church member]; he might know. Things I don't know, I ask him. Things he don't know he ask me.

(On the phone with friend and fellow church member Jesse Blackmon)
But when that killing happened down there on 18th Street. I don't know
what year that was. You know. Well, you never used to go, but I used to
go get peanuts. We used to go down there to that union. I remember
him very well. Bet Willie would have known. Well, I was talking to a
friend of mine [Lester] and telling him about what had happened down
there. Yeah, City Inspector. Poured out every Monday til the man stopped
him. No, they killed him down there, tied his body to the back of the
patrol and dragged him through town. Somebody, a rich white woman
said, "Cut him loose. You done killed him. That's enough!" That was a
big thing, a really big thing. Okay, then his wife knew the man's daughter.

(Off phone) I knew the incident. The white man had a place, what you
called a marketplace, and you sold peanuts. Now you get so much out
of what you sell. You know those little sacks full of peanuts; they still
come in those little sacks. You'd go down there and they would have
already stacked them up for you. When they stacked them up, they would
give you so many bags, 30 or 40, and you'd get so much out. Sometimes
you wouldn't sell them all. I used to take them to anywhere there was a
crowd. If I knew where a crowd was, I would try to sell them all day.
Folks buy them peanuts too. Only nickel a bag, you could do pretty good.
Just a little money—something like a dollar to two—that was big money.
Right on 49th Street was a place called the Daily Club. It's a white folks
club, and on the other side of the alley was where a white woman lived.
I was going on my way to the club and she said, "Hey boy! Boy!" I was
going right by her door. She said, "You want a job making some money?"
"Yes, ma'am." "Come on around here," and I did, and she told me what
she wanted me to do: roll a lot of ashes outside of the basement, look
like they had been there I don't know how many winters. She said, "I'll
pay you good." So I rolled all those ashes out, and she gave a quarter. A
quarter! Now if I don't like something, I usually say something about it,
but there is a time to talk and a time to listen. And back then, the most
of the time was to listen. I said, "Is this all you gonna pay me?" I believe
you would have said the same thing. I don't know how many ashes was
in that basement. She had an old wheel barrel; that was what I would
load them up and then carry them out. Come back, go back in there and
do that again. It was no quarter job, wasn't no dollar job, but I figured
she might give me a dollar. If she gave me a dollar I might not go to the
club. I might go on back home, play a little golf myself, knock a few balls
around. She said, "Do you want that quarter?" I said, "Yes ma'am, but I
thought you would pay me a little more than a quarter." She said, "I
paid you a quarter and that is all I am going to pay you. Now you get on
away from here." Said, "Do you want to get on away from here or do

you want me to call the police on you?" I said, "I want to get on away from here." And I got on away from there. Boy I am telling you that hurts me. I will never forget about that. I believe if I went crazy, I'd think about that. That woman, the way that she would give me a quarter and then threaten me with the law. You see the police whup [beat] black folks.

LESTER: So it wasn't just a matter of being locked up? You were whupped [beaten] and then locked up?

HENDERSON: That's right. That's just the way things were.

TOPICS FOR WRITTEN OR ORAL DISCUSSION: HENDERSON INTERVIEW

1. Discuss the significance of present and past tense shifts in Henderson's interview.

2. Discuss Henderson's interview as a series of short stories or narratives.

3. Cite examples of storytelling rhetoric.

4. Discuss the significance of repetitions in the interview.

5. Identify and discuss the significance of family rituals in the interview.

6. Discuss Henderson's meticulous attention to place details in the interview.

7. Discuss the episodes of violence in the interview.

8. Discuss the significance of names and naming in the interview.

9. Discuss instances of blurred past and present in terms of black-white race relations mentioned in the interview.

10. Identify and discuss the examples of folklore in the interview.

11. Discuss the interviewee's mood shifts that occur during the different parts of the interview. How are these mood shifts about certain aspects of his details reflected in the language he uses to tell his stories?

12. How does Henderson define the blues? Compare Henderson's definition to Hurston's presentation in *Their Eyes Were Watching God*.

13. Compare Henderson's specifics about gender roles to Hurston's presentation in *Their Eyes Were Watching God*.

14. At one point in the interview, Henderson says that "You know when you scared, you gonna pray." Discuss this comment in its context, and compare its meanings to the moment in the novel when the characters are humbled by their fear of the life-threatening hurricane.

15. Discuss Henderson's variations on playing the dozens—ritual of in-

sults that involves verbal sparring and finesse, usually a competition between males.

16. Research the blues singers Henderson mentions. What were their songs about? Compare their songs to Hurston's presentation of the blues motif in *Their Eyes Were Watching God*.

I had not met John and Lizzie Marshall before this interview. In fact, my barber, after hearing of my research on the life of southern blacks during the 1920s and 1930s, introduced me to this delightful couple, who were more than willing to share their experiences. Their interview offers a view of life from the perspective of a married black couple.

In discussing their lives, the Marshalls offer details concerning educational opportunities for blacks and details concerning blacks' economic situation. Amid details of the treatment of blacks by such political figures as Eugene "Bull" Connor, the Birmingham police commissioner who gained notoriety during the spring of 1963 by turning power hoses and police dogs on black demonstrators protesting for their civil rights, the Marshalls gladly sprinkle in details that celebrate their youthful romance. They also touch on intraracism among African Americans.

INTERVIEW WITH JOHN AND LIZZIE MARSHALL, CONDUCTED AT THEIR HOME IN BIRMINGHAM, ALABAMA (JUNE 15, 1996)

LESTER: Let me start by getting your full names.

LIZZIE MARSHALL: Lizzie Crawford Marshall.

LESTER: And you, sir?

JOHN MARSHALL: John E. Marshall.

LESTER: When were you born?

LIZZIE MARSHALL: Well, I will tell you, 1909.

JOHN MARSHALL: 10–29–1914. I am eighty-one.

LESTER: And were you both born in the South?

LIZZIE MARSHALL: Utah, Alabama.

JOHN MARSHALL: I was born in Jefferson County, eight miles from Jefferson County Court House.

LESTER: Did you grow up and spend all your time here in the South?

JOHN MARSHALL: Other than being in the army.

LESTER: When were you in the army? World War II?

JOHN MARSHALL: That's right. I spent a little over two years in the medics.

LIZZIE MARSHALL: You know, I had three sisters born before me, and my mom couldn't read and write at that time. So she and my great aunt, my great, great aunt, they got into a fuss about my age, but my great aunt said 1915, and my mama said 1909. So there I got a problem. I just say 1909, or what they call 09.

JOHN MARSHALL: I was born by the midwife; that's history too.

LIZZIE MARSHALL: So on my identification, it says 1915. But I know all of that goes along.

LESTER: Tell me about you two getting married. When did you get married?

LIZZIE MARSHALL: Let's see, I was married before him. Let me tell you I had a hard time before I got married. I had just finished high school, and I had sought college work at Alabama State [University]. And so they went on and hired me with this man. I used to be his secretary, take the names and all. I was real young when I got that, real young. Lord, have mercy! And so, I had to marry, and I got this man [not John Marshall], and he was a gentleman from his heart, and I loved him, I thought. And he would go out and I wouldn't want that, so after that, I separated. My mama went to Wisconsin, and she lived up there 'cause I had a baby. So all that is what that's all about. Then I met him [John Marshall], and he was such a wonderful man, and we finally got ourselves married.

Before that, I had a hard time. I had three girls by the same man. One named Lori Jean, the next one's Mary, and the next is Novell, and I had a hard time.

LESTER: Well, what was that life like?

LIZZIE MARSHALL: I said, "Lord, have mercy!" We lived across the street from a white lady that was friends with my mama. This lady was married to a rich man. He made nine hundred dollars a month. We thought that was big money, so he was rich. So she would help us out, help my mama out. And after she did that every time I was pregnant, she would have her children bring some food over because I was pregnant. Alright, here is what I say, "Lord, I got to get out here and go to work." I was a little thin thing. I wasn't tall, wasn't as tall as I am now. I grew taller as I grew older. After I did that, I finished school. Then I finished college. And I asked for some work—washing and ironing, cleaning up, whatever—I will be glad to. So she said, "Alright, I have a baby in here, and I would like you to take care of her." I said, "Yes, ma'am." I said, "I sure will. I'll wash. I was boiling clothes in the pot, would put some lye in there to make them smell good. I started to iron, stiffen her husband's shirt 'cause they liked them stiff. And you got to get those charcoals to heat that iron with, and I did those things real good. She wasn't able to pay too much, but I didn't let her down 'cause she took me in first.

Then I went to another lady's house, and I left my little children with someone for a while so that I could work. So I went to another lady's. I wanted more money. So I went to her house, and she said, "I don't have no money, but I have some peas in here." I said, "Well, I need some meat with the peas." That's the truth! And I washed. It made me be a woman. It made me be a woman.

LESTER: Tell me about your schooling. Was going to college rather uncommon?

LIZZIE MARSHALL: They don't charge nothing for high school; they don't charge nothing.

LESTER: But you said you went to Alabama State.

LIZZIE MARSHALL: I don't know what that was, my mama paid that. And I had aunties who'd take me to school. I was just wild. My daddy was a coal miner.

LESTER: You were raised by your mom? And then you raised your daughter. And then Mr. John came along.

LIZZIE MARSHALL: Yeah. Mr. John came along. So after he came . . .

LESTER: What year was that?

JOHN MARSHALL: It was in the 1930s.

LESTER: Did you meet in Birmingham?

JOHN MARSHALL: Cleveland they call it, Cleveland State.

LESTER: And you have been married about sixty years?

LIZZIE MARSHALL: Yeah, and his ma didn't want him to marry. But after that, we would go out and get married. If the girls liked him, I had that problem. (*Laughs*) But that's alright.

LESTER: I bet you [Lizzie Marshall] were popular.

JOHN MARSHALL: Yeah. She was popular. She could play the piano. In fact, we donated our piano to the church, our church right here. What she was playing was big-fat-mama-rough-type music. She was not playing no religious songs.

LIZZIE MARSHALL: Now after that, I got baptized—when I was 9 years old.

LESTER: Tell me about some of that blues music.

LIZZIE MARSHALL: "Sweet old Kokomo." (*Sings*)

JOHN MARSHALL: (Sings)

LESTER: And it was okay for women to sing the blues? I know it was really popular.

JOHN MARSHALL: Yeah, they used to have places like that. Back in Fats Waller—we were back in his days. What were some of his songs?

LIZZIE MARSHALL: All I know was everybody said, "Come on and play Kokomo."

JOHN MARSHALL: The Charleston was the dance back then.

LESTER: Oh, the Charleston. Well, where would black people go back for dancing and recreation?

JOHN MARSHALL: In the houses.

LIZZIE MARSHALL: Oh, there were places we were able to go.

JOHN MARSHALL: Just a short way from here was a place called the Dugout. And people would say, "I am going to the Dugout." Yeah, people do same thing today.

LESTER: Rent parties, charge twenty-five cents or something, and after a while you have your rent, right?

LIZZIE MARSHALL: Yeah, and have a good time in the process. And one thing with those people, if you didn't have, I had. People in our day made us be closer. When I was pregnant, there was this lady who said, "Lizzie, come over here." Telephone, child I didn't even know how to use a telephone. It was about this tall, and mama said go down to the store and here's a nickel and call on the phone. And so I would call. It took a whole lot longer than today, and the number was only 094, not like today. He [unidentified person] he had a store.

JOHN MARSHALL: He [unidentified] had a store across the street. That was an American white man. And you buy a dime's worth of liver, and tell the man to give you some lard.

LIZZIE MARSHALL: And that was good food too, not what it is now.

LESTER: Did you ever make any lard?

LIZZIE MARSHALL: Yeah, it might look like lard when you see it, but you get some corn bread mix and stir it in there.

JOHN MARSHALL: But you had to heat it up. It'll change colors while you heat it.

LIZZIE MARSHALL: And if you could buy a dime's worth of liver . . .

JOHN MARSHALL: Tell the man to give you a little onion, and you make gravy and it go over the grits.

LIZZIE MARSHALL: That's true, child!

LESTER: Sounds like a good meal.

LIZZIE MARSHALL: These foods we're talking about here were good and solid. They keep you well.

We were young and we didn't have nothing, John and I didn't. But they [unidentified] would take me and John everywhere they went. John would cut up and they liked it. John still had curly hair. He thought he was something. It was about your color, but curly black hair. And he was pretty with that. And his girlfriend—she had a pretty big house. So every time they did something, they [unidentified] would invite me and John. And so, she [John's girlfriend's family] had a piano, so they invited us there, and when we got there, they said, here's Lizzie, come on and play. And so we had got married there, and as soon as we got there, a boy jumped up and kissed me, and John slapped him down on the floor.

LESTER: That man was out of order, wasn't he?

LIZZIE MARSHALL: Well, but he didn't know. He said, "She is my wife." But nobody had told him I was his wife.

JOHN MARSHALL: You don't go around explaining nothing. You don't go around taking over.

LIZZIE MARSHALL: Isn't he terrible? Anyway, we were young and wild. We went to a club party at one of the places we called the Dugout. We would come out and we would have the dances in the basement, called it the Dugout. A lot of the clubs would have their dances in the basement. The Dugout was a beautiful place; it was so pretty. John couldn't go out much 'cause his mama was always watching him. Tell him what your mama said. I'll tell it. He always get out the window and come over to my house. That's the truth. He'd come on over there and stay a while. His mama caught him coming out the window, and so she said, "John!" And he said, "Mama." She said, "What you doing?" And he said, "Ma'am, I don't know." (*Laughs*) I declare. And we laughed when we found out 'cause she caught him there.

LESTER: He sounds like he was a joker.

LIZZIE MARSHALL: He was coming over to my house, and I was going to go over to the park.

LESTER: I see.

JOHN MARSHALL: I was going to slip out of the house. That's the house right there, third house on the other side of this one.

LESTER: Really?

JOHN MARSHALL: That house was built in '29.

LESTER: Tell me what life was like growing up and living in the South in the twenties and thirties.

LIZZIE MARSHALL: Nobody had nothing. Nobody was rich. Everybody had mostly food to eat and if you had something to wear—Lord, you don't know—talking about hard. What was that, the recession? But I am here to tell you people loved one another more.

JOHN MARSHALL: I had two brothers and two sisters. How many is that?

LESTER: Four, wait, you've got two brothers and sisters.

JOHN MARSHALL: Lot of folks don't do no counting like you do. You missed the mark. I've still got two brothers and sisters.

LESTER: Black people knew their places?

JOHN MARSHALL: White folks totally agree. "Nigger, you ain't done! You ain't counting!"

LIZZIE MARSHALL: When I would go to work, it would be time to eat. They would give me some butter beans and some biscuits and tell me to sit on the porch steps there and eat it.

JOHN MARSHALL: Made you come in the back door and things.

LIZZIE MARSHALL: You know they just started this back since that lady— you know her in your lifetime—you know the lady that didn't want to sit on the backseat.

LESTER: Rosa Parks.

LIZZIE MARSHALL: That's when that came.

JOHN MARSHALL: That's later years.

LESTER: Did people just accept that reality, or were people challenging that?

LIZZIE MARSHALL: You have to accept it.

JOHN MARSHALL: They called you "nigger," and at that time, and you was a "nigger."

LIZZIE MARSHALL: "Tell that nigger to get on out there on that porch and sweep."

LESTER: The men and the women were treated the same?

LIZZIE MARSHALL: What you talking about?

LESTER: Mistreated the same?

JOHN MARSHALL: Rosa Parks stuck her neck out, and thank God she is still making history. This 16th Street Baptist Church bombing [1963] woke up a lot of things. And another thing, the Peterson case, that was in Scottsboro, that was a history. Some of them older folks was still living. They killed some. They put some Negroes in jail and that kind of stuff. The Peterson case that was the case of the cases for Negroes. Bull Connor used to sic dogs on you and all that kind of stuff. Bull Connor didn't want Negroes in his house, but one worked for him. He left home at eight o'clock in the morning, and the maid couldn't get there til nine. So he never did see her. And that's right here on 56th Street. He got in his yard a black bull. That's where "Bull" Connor comes from.

LIZZIE MARSHALL: Like the little black boy with a white hat on, the bull is sitting in the yard. You pass that way, don't you?

LESTER: I live over in that area, so I'll have to check on that.

JOHN MARSHALL: When you get to 56th Street, you turn left, go one block. That's where Bull Connor used to live and there is a black bull there now.

LIZZIE MARSHALL: No, it's a little black boy with a white hat and white pants and a red shirt.

LESTER: Before that time, were cemeteries, and churches and waiting rooms and all that segregated?

JOHN MARSHALL: Teal was the first Negro to be out in an integrated cemetery. And I was working at Bowling Flower Shop when they put Teal from Grace Hill to Bauchalomb Cemetery. Coming down 6th Avenue, that was the first Negro ever put into a military graveyard.

LESTER: And that in the thirties?

JOHN MARSHALL: No, that was later than the thirties.

LIZZIE MARSHALL: 'Cause when you was coming to town, I didn't know the way to town. You talking about a country girl.

JOHN MARSHALL: When they moved that body, when the body had been dead, guy named Teal and Sandra's boyfriend. And they lived on 1st Avenue, near the Miller place. As you go down that avenue, that's where Teal was living. That was a sight, to see someone pulled, from one cemetery and put him in another cemetery. And I was looking at the eye of the funeral when the funeral was going on.

LESTER: But why did they do that? Why would they pull him?

JOHN MARSHALL: He had made a vow within himself that when he died he wanted to be buried at Avenue F. They didn't bury him there at the present time. They had put him in Grace Hill, but then they had to dig him up and bring him down to Avenue F, which was then 6th Avenue.

LIZZIE MARSHALL: Our granddaughter was in the same cemetery. She was Catholic. One thing them white women teach—what do they call them white women?

JOHN MARSHALL: The nuns?

LIZZIE MARSHALL: Yeah, 'cause one of those women, she was over here, not too long ago. The nun, she calls me because the teacher of this school, she said, the boys liked her, so whatever she told them to do, they loved to do, and you know. So after then, the teacher, Mrs. White, did something to Sandra, my granddaughter, and she called me and told me not to say nothing about it, 'cause it was her fault, the teacher's fault not hers. And those boys said, "If you fuss at Sandra again, we gonna beat you up." They told the teacher that. And they said she fussed at Sandra too much. They didn't say that she beat her up. The nun called me up that night and said, "Honey girl, that wasn't true." Her husband, he was the director of music, and here's what happened. He had this car give him trouble. He did the best he could, so it caught on fire. She said, "You know what?" She told the man that told her husband. She told her husband that because of the fact that it did run, so she said, and the nun called me and said, "Mrs. Marshall, you know that your daughter's got plenty devil in her." That's true, she said that.

JOHN MARSHALL: She's what you call a high yellow back then.

LIZZIE MARSHALL: Child done everything she said, that's true. I ain't gonna tell no lie. So she said, "Mrs. Marshall." So I said, "What did she do?" The teacher, Mrs. White, the nun called me. She said that the teacher has called in sick twice 'cause of those boys, because of Sandra, and she says, "She's the devil." So I said, "No, my daughter plays with me, teaches music. She's with me on my Sunday playing and singing." You know she plays the organ or piano, whatever I want her to play. She teaches music. She don't have time for nothing like that. The man was a director of music in some school, and it was of course all messed up. You understand. Well the wire caught fire or something, you know old cars they do that. So they said, "I tried to fix that." She didn't do that, or the boys either. And that fixed that, but I just got upset because I felt that they were jealous of her, so that's what she told me. These teachers now, they was hard on the black children. They segregated them schools. They still do.

LESTER: You told me earlier about violence you witnessed. What had the person done?

LIZZIE MARSHALL: See the boy wanted some water. John Henry sings about it. I got his picture in there.

LESTER: Tell me something about the violence you witnessed. Did you experience any?

LIZZIE MARSHALL: I saw it when I was a little girl. I don't know how long. I remember that man with a long whip.

JOHN MARSHALL: Early thirties.

LESTER: Tell me about what that must have been like.

JOHN MARSHALL: It's Captain Power. That was in the earlier thirties, like the ball and chains like they're trying to use now.

LESTER: Chain gangs?

JOHN MARSHALL: Yeah, chain gangs. Captain Power.

LESTER: What is Captain Power?

JOHN MARSHALL: He had the power over the prisoners. The chain gangs they use now aren't no chain gangs.

LESTER: It was much worse then?

JOHN MARSHALL: They had a ball and chain hooked on to them.

LIZZIE MARSHALL: It was big, hanging on to them, and if they didn't get that thing along, they had a long whip about this long, and that man would say, "I'm a gonna whip you!" Man, I was a little girl and I can see that now. Boy, can I see that. And Captain Power had a white hat.

LESTER: This was here in Birmingham?

LIZZIE MARSHALL: Yeah! I tell you it was dangerous. I was a little girl and I didn't like that—seeing a grown man being whipped.

JOHN MARSHALL: That was in '44.

LIZZIE MARSHALL: They was working on that train rail. They had to work all along them, take them apart, rebuild them and oil them—the tracks.

JOHN MARSHALL: That was before the Amtrak.

LIZZIE MARSHALL: And it was a hot summer.

LESTER: Well, what about day-to-day life? Were black people threatened all the time?

LIZZIE MARSHALL: They take the white man's word first. And if two people, a white man was into something, and the colored man was there, the colored man stole it " 'cause that's a 'nigger.' "

LESTER: So there was no justice there?

LIZZIE MARSHALL: No, one time, someone said, "I know that lady [white]." He said that she was pretty and they [whites] wanted to hang him. Remember, John? We were downtown and they were looking for that man. We were sitting in the car and it was a place where you could do it. They were looking for him to lynch him.

LESTER: So was this a day-to-day reality—that lynching could occur at any time over virtually anything?

LIZZIE MARSHALL: If they'd a got that boy, they would have hung him.

LESTER: Did you witness that or just hear people talking about it? Did you witness any lynchings?

JOHN MARSHALL: We was around.

LIZZIE MARSHALL: We wouldn't be around something like that, white folks beating on black folks. Mama and daddy together and I was just mad!

LESTER: How did your parents respond to that?

LIZZIE MARSHALL: I can't remember.

LESTER: Did they talk to you much about it?

LIZZIE MARSHALL: No.

LESTER: About what not to do?

JOHN MARSHALL: Oh, you did not go out to town or be caught out in town.

LESTER: So that was spelled out by your parents? And everybody knew that?

JOHN MARSHALL: And let me tell you another thing. In that house over there just like our house right here, houses had fences and gates and the family was restricted to be in before dark. The kids wasn't accounted for if they wasn't in before the sun went down. You were not accounted for if you were not in the gate before sundown.

LIZZIE MARSHALL: They don't do that now.

LESTER: Tell me a little bit about your education.

JOHN MARSHALL: I went three and a half years of high school, but I really didn't drop out. I went to industrial school.

LIZZIE MARSHALL: He took some trades.

LESTER: What did you do?

JOHN MARSHALL: I took up upholstering and repair down here when they had night school. In fact, I used to teach class.

LESTER: How long did you do that?

JOHN MARSHALL: Upholstery and repair, I did that when G.I. training come into technical college. At that time, the situation was that he'd give you a salary and the government would give you a supplement. But I stopped that 'cause I knowed that wasn't long and I didn't get a certificate. But I knowed more about it than the teacher, teacher named Clark, the training school at night, but I learned more about what I know in practice. See, they wouldn't hire a lot of times unless you had a high school education. And I had papers.

LIZZIE MARSHALL: But let me tell you what they did to me. I went semesters during the summertime. I was young. I finished at an early age.

LESTER: When did you learn to play the piano?

JOHN MARSHALL: Just a gift.

LIZZIE MARSHALL: I took some notes in Paris, Texas.

JOHN MARSHALL: She traveled with me. I didn't go overseas during the war. I spent all my time in the States, and she traveled with me.

LESTER: Was segregation in the army at that time?

JOHN MARSHALL: It was a little bit different.

LESTER: Not as bad?

JOHN MARSHALL: It was cooling down.

LESTER: Tell me about the role of the church and religion for black folks during the 1920's and 30's. When all of these other kinds of things were threatening, where was church during all of this?

LIZZIE MARSHALL: You stayed in your own church. In those days, I didn't see any black folk unless you cleaning it up, or washing the dishes as everyone else is getting ready to go home. Now that's your job.

JOHN MARSHALL: You know they wanted to send a nigger over there to that place. And that place is where the white folks designated him to be.

LIZZIE MARSHALL: Don't you see these black churches burning up? They wanted it to be like that long time ago.

LESTER: Was the KKK doing some of that then?

JOHN MARSHALL: I think they still doing it.

LESTER: So it wasn't uncommon to see KKK riding up and down the streets?

LIZZIE MARSHALL: They doing it now.

JOHN MARSHALL: Peterson, Scottsboro, you ought to know a little bit about it.

LESTER: I know about the Scottsboro boys.

JOHN MARSHALL: Yeah, that's what I was talking about.

LESTER: Yeah, I teach the book based on that case. [In 1931, nine black boys (ages 13–20) in Scottsboro, Alabama were wrongly accused of raping two white women. After a series of mistrials and appeals that lasted more than a decade, the men were released or pardoned.]

LIZZIE MARSHALL: You do?

LESTER: Yes, I teach *To Kill a Mockingbird*, which is based on that.

LIZZIE MARSHALL: The lady at the Scottsboro, she worked at Brumberg's. We worked there together. I can't think of her name. She is a beautiful girl—very kind and nice—but I don't know how they did that to her. She loved black and white. She was kind. What did they do to him? What was his name?

JOHN MARSHALL: Peterson, wasn't it?

LIZZIE MARSHALL: Sounds like it.

LESTER: Was it hard for you to get a job at Bromberg's?

LIZZIE MARSHALL: No, I had an aunt that had worked there for years.

LESTER: So were people really taken with skin color back then?

LIZZIE MARSHALL: Oh, you better hush!

LESTER: Was it the lighter you were, the better?

JOHN MARSHALL: In industrial, they had what they called a yellow hammer, and if you wasn't yellow hammer you couldn't get no position in industrial. They had a guy named Wilkinson, and he was as dark, and I don't think he had any family. *(Phone rings)*

The biggest job was to find out who I was working with and who I could rely on. I had zoned, before there was zoning, this warehouse behind that yellow building that you see out there. And I zoned it off, put it in my mind, and if anybody come in I would say something like, "Go to Zone Six." And I would say, "Cut the lights out. I don't want the lights on." I could find anything in that warehouse 'cause I had it in my mind, but the guy I worked with couldn't do that. But the bossman himself retired and they made me a shipping clerk, over about twelve men.

LESTER: When was this?

JOHN MARSHALL: That was about 1938 until about 1968, about thirty something years. I was the shipping clerk. The other guy, he could rub it in. "But Mr. Marshall will be with you." And I will say, "You're early. You're not supposed to be here, but I'll be with you." Now I am a nigger talking here. They looking for a white man. Those things still exist. But I was the man, the only one with a key to the warehouse. And one morning I was in Franklin, Kentucky, and supposed to be at a wedding. I was 199 miles away and they had to have a key made to get into the warehouse 'cause I was the only one that had a key. And the white man that owned the place, and he didn't come til late that afternoon. They had to get a locksmith. And I was her [Lizzy's] bossman. She worked there too.

LIZZIE MARSHALL: Not really with him. I was working in the office with the white girls.

JOHN MARSHALL: I also had a job where I entertained the veterans, but they came giving me only something to get me on aid [financial], and I didn't want to get on the aid; we have too many already on aid.

A man used to come around in our time named Jamison, who would give you a medicine that was good for everything—constipation and everything.

LESTER: But what did people know about doctors?

LIZZIE MARSHALL: We used to take a drop or two of turpentine, or take medicine.

JOHN MARSHALL: The old powdered black dog.

LESTER: People were healthier?

LIZZIE MARSHALL: Yeah, making margarine. It looked kinda like a log, and it had a little coloring.

JOHN MARSHALL: What about that cinnamon that grows on trees?

LESTER: I've not seen any of that.

JOHN MARSHALL: It turned your mouth.

LESTER: Sounds like you had a great sense of community. People looked out for each other.

LIZZIE MARSHALL: Do you know how many grandchildren we have? I have five grand, grandchildren. In fact I am in the fourth generation. (*Talks with a visiting adult grandchild*)

LESTER: Four generations. And what did your mother do to live to be a hundred? You've got to do something right.

JOHN MARSHALL: Singing in the choir.

LESTER: Sounds like I am seeing some of her in you.

LIZZIE MARSHALL: My father was 7'2" and my mother was 5'5".

LESTER: 7'2"—that was an unusual height.

TOPICS FOR WRITTEN OR ORAL EXPLORATION: MARSHALL INTERVIEW

1. Discuss details about education for blacks according to the Marshalls.

2. How are the Marshalls' stories individually quite different?

3. What story do you think Lizzie Marshall is most interested in sharing? Why?

4. What are the differences between John Marshall's responses to the interview questions and Lizzie's?

5. What parallels and differences do you see in the details provided in Joseph Henderson's interview and this interview with the Marshalls?

6. Which details from these interviews reinforce the life experiences of blacks depicted in *Their Eyes Were Watching God*?

HURSTON'S HOMETOWN

Today, Eatonville, Florida, about ten miles northeast of downtown Orlando, draws international visitors who are curious about the place that nurtured Zora Neale Hurston. Eatonville and Hurston's legacy are being preserved and celebrated by such organizations as the Association to Preserve the Eatonville Community, Incorporated (227 East Kennedy Boulevard, Eatonville, FL 32751), and the Town of Eatonville (332 East Kennedy Boulevard, Eatonville, FL 32751). There is also an annual Zora! Festival that attracts scholars and communities nourished by the life of Zora Neale Hurston. No efforts have been made to edit the following essays grammatically or stylistically.

This advertisement appeared on the front page of Eatonville's weekly newspaper, *The Eatonville Speaker*, on January 22, 1889. In an effort to attract blacks to Eatonville, the announcement promises a segregated refuge from white people and racism. Hurston details Jody Clarke's creation of the all-black, self-governing township in *Their Eyes Were Watching God*.

Students might look at the histories of other all-black settlements such as the Nicodemus, Kansas Movement of 1877 where ex-slaves were invited to settle to escape Southern white racism after the Civil War. Public flyers were also distributed widely to encourage the westward migration of 20,000–40,000 blacks from the south to Kansas.

THE EATONVILLE SPEAKER, "EATONVILLE, FLORIDA: *THE NATION'S OLDEST BLACK INCORPORATED MUNICIPALITY*" (JANUARY 22, 1889)

Colored people of the United States: Solve the great race problem by securing a home in Eatonville, Florida, a Negro city governed by negroes.

Eatonville, Orange County, Florida, is situated six miles north of Orlando, the County seat of Orange County, two miles north of Winter Park and a half-mile north of park house station and places that are noted winter resorts. Winter Park being the location of the far-famed Seminole Hotel. During the years between 1875–1877 an effort was made by Allen

Ricket, J.E. Clarke and another colored man to purchase land for the purpose of establishing a colony for colored people, but so great was the prejudice then existing against the Negroe that no one would sell the land for such a purpose. In 1883, Lewis Lawrence, who came to Maitland in 1875 from Utica, New York, came to the rescue by purchasing the land on which is now the Town of Eatonville, named after a Mr. Eaton. Mr. Lawrence, who at once built them a church and several cottages, gave them a chance to pay for the same on easy payments. Tony Taylor and Allen Ricket were the first to take up their residence in Eatonville. Six years have passed and today Eatonville is an incorporated city of between two and three hundred population with a Mayor, Board of Aldermen, and all the necessary adjuncts of a full-fledged city, all colored, and not a white family in the whole city!

Five and ten tracts can be bought for five and ten dollars an acre, according to location and improvements. In Eatonville, lots to actual settlers (colored): 44 × 100, can be bought for thiry-five dollars cash; and fifty on time.

Zora Neale Hurston acts as a lively tour guide for those arriving in Eatonville, Florida. Her description of the place she knows intimately allows readers of her fiction generally and of *Their Eyes Were Watching God* in particular to better visualize and situate the narrative actions. Showing that cultural and individual identities are products of physical places—Florida Everglades, West Florida, Maitland, Eatonville, Jacksonville, Palm Beach, Fort Myers, and Fort Lauderdale spatially punctuate the novel—Hurston's account here is a map drawn by one who almost single-handedly put Eatonville, Florida, on the literary map of the world. Unlike William Faulkner's fictitious creation and peopling of Yoknapatawpha County, Hurston's presentation of Eatonville, Florida is real and immediate.

ZORA NEALE HURSTON, "EATONVILLE: WHEN YOU LOOK AT IT" (OCTOBER 1, 1938)

Maitland is Maitland until it gets to Hurst's corner, and then it is Eatonville. Right in front of Willie Sewell's yellow-painted house the hard road quits being the hard road for a generous mile and becomes the heart of Eatonville. Or from a stranger's point of view, you could say that the road just burst through on its way from Highway #17 to #441 scattering Eatonville right and left.

On the right after you leave the Sewell place you don't meet a thing that people live in until you come to the Green Lantern on the main corner. That corner has always been the main corner because that is where Joe Clarke, the founder and first mayor of Eatonville, built his store when he started the town nearly sixty years ago, so that people have gotten used to gathering there and talking. Only Joe Clarke sold groceries and general merchandise, while Lee Glenn sells drinks and whatever goes with transient rooms. St. Lawrence Methodist church and parsonage are on that same side of the road between Sewells and "the shop" and perhaps claim the soul of the place, but the shop is the heart of it. After the shop you come to Widow Dash's orange grove, her screened porch, "double hips" and her new husband. Way down the end of the road to the right is Claude Mann's filling station and beyond that the last house in Eatonville, the big barn on the lake that is lived in by Zora Neale Hurston.

Take the left side of the road and except for Macedonia Baptist church, people just live along that side and play croquet in Armetta Jones' back-yard behind the huge camphor tree. After the people quit living along that side of the road, The Robert Hungerford Industrial School begins and runs along the road for some distance so far as the land goes. The inadequate buildings stop short in the cleared land on the fringe of Eatonville proper. And west of it all, village and school, everybody knows that the sun makes his nest in some lonesome lake in the woods back there and gets his night rest.

But all of Eatonville is not on the hard road that becomes Apopka Avenue as it passes through town. There are back streets on both sides of the road. The two back streets on the right side are full of little houses squatting under hovering oaks. These houses are old and were made out of the town's first dreams. There is loved Lake Sabelia with its small colpony of very modern houses lived in by successful villagers like Kelly Baldwin and the Williams. Away in the woody rises beyond Lake Sabelia is Eatonville's Dogtown that looks as if it belonged on the African veldt. Off the road in the left is the brown with white trim modern public school with its well kept yards and playgrounds that Howard Miller always looks after though he can scarcely read and write. They call this part of town Mars Hill as against Bones Valley to the right of the hard road. They call the tree-shaded lane that runs past the schoolhouse West Street and it goes past several minor groves until it passes Jim Steel's fine orange grove and dips itself into Lake Belle, which is the home of Eatonville's most celebrated resident, the world's largest alligator.

5

"Singing and Sobbing": The Blues Tradition

As there are common misconceptions about Negro spirituals, there are also misconceptions about the blues, another African American folk tradition centering on orality and self-creation. In fact, the primary misconception about spirituals and the blues is that they are sad and depressing. Out of sadness, disillusionment, disappointment, and oppression, spirituals and blues emerge. The songs' movements toward hopefulness, however, ultimately define these two aesthetically related folksong genres and traditions. Turn-of-the-century essayist and social critic W.E.B. Du Bois's words about spirituals in *The Souls of Black Folk* (1903) can easily be linked to the blues:

> These [sorrow] songs are the articulate message of the slave to the world. . . . They are the music of an unhappy people, of the children of disappointment; they tell of death and suffering and unvoiced longing toward a truer world, of misty wanderings and hidden ways. . . .
>
> Through all the sorrow of the Sorrow Songs there breathes a hope—a faith in the ultimate justice of things.[1]

Created by slaves who were denied literacy, spirituals document the power of self-fashioning, of slaves redefining themselves not as masters' animals but as human beings fully capable of complex verbal creations and communications. Transferring the biblical stories of heroic victories preached to them by plantation evangelists, slaves put themselves on an equal plane with the characters, insisting in song that if "My Lord delivered Daniel from the lions' den, Jonah from the belly of the whale, and the Hebrew boys from the fiery furnace," the Lord would surely deliver them from their bondage and suffering as well. This explains the hopefulness in such tunes as "Swing Low, Sweet Chariot," "Sometimes I Feel Like a Motherless Child," "Steal Away," and "There Is a Balm in Gilead."

The blues are not exactly mirror images of the spirituals. The blues are indeed secular, although rhythms, themes, and aesthetics of the music provide remarkable parallels with gospel music. The blues are expressions of the *folk*, not necessarily the educated, learned black people. The blues bemoan the hardships of life with a raw emotion that consumes listeners with an almost religious fervor. And while the blues lament the pains of living and loving, they are ultimately spoken testimonials of survival, of celebrations of life and living despite the hard knocks and disappointments. To sing about the pain is to survive the pain; silence would acknowledge defeat. Filled with ambivalence and emotion—in love but lovesick, in love but with a married man, in love but he's not around—the blues express a state of mind. A random sampling of Bessie Smith song titles alone signals the range of blues perspectives: "Crazy Blues," "Down Hearted Blues," "Sweet Black Woman," "Rocking Chair Blues," "Jailhouse Blues," "Sobbin' Hearted Blues," "Dirty No-Gooder's Blues," "Down in the Dumps," "In the House Blues," "Shipwreck Blues," "Take Me for a Buggy Ride," "Blue Blues," "Wasted Life Blues," "Standin' in the Rain Blues," "Baby Won't You Please Come Home," "Pick Pocket Blues," "Backwater Blues," "Young Woman's Blues," "Mean Ole Bedbug Blues," "Nobody Knows You When You Down and Out," "Please Help Me Get Him off My Mind," "Reckless Blues," "My Man Blues," "Poor Man's Blues," "Empty Bed Blues," "Give Me a Pigfoot," and "Hard Time Blues." The blues convey creativity from despair, sexual satisfaction, and empty beds together in one utterance. Unlike the more controlled and urban jazz creations, the blues are rural, low-down, sexual, raunchy, teasing, guttural expressions of African American realities that blur the lines between god and human beings, religious and secular, sensual and sacred.

Janie's entire story is a blues text. As she tells her story of pain and suffering to Phoeby and subsequently to the other porch-sitters through Phoeby and to the reading audience, Janie does not lament a life not lived. In fact, her life is celebration. At the novel's end when she has time to reflect on all the passion and pain she has experienced in her quest for love and spiritual companionship, Janie philosophizes: "Ah done been tuh de horizon and back and now Ah kin set heah in mah house and live by comparisons" (*TEWWG* 284–285).

Although various characters in *Their Eyes Were Watching God* contribute to blues moments, the novel is ultimately Janie's song, a black woman's blues. As such, the greatest pain from Janie's life comes in loving and losing Tea Cake, the man who "held de keys tuh da kingdom" for her and embodied "the love thoughts of women." Such a blues moment occurs when Tea Cake takes Janie's money unbeknownst to her and stays out all night. The novel's narrator expresses Janie's thoughts on loving Tea Cake and being in love:

> In the cool of the afternoon, the fiend from hell specially sent to lovers arrived at Janie's ear. Doubt. All the fears that circumstance could provide and the heart feel, attacked her on every side. . . .
>   She adored him [Tea Cake] and hated him at the same time. How could he make her suffer so and then come grinning like that with that darling way he had? (*TEWWG* 163–164)

Janie also sings the blues in her relationship with Nanny. The novel introduces Leafy's and parts of Nanny's stories as blues texts. In contrast, Mrs. Turner's lamentations are caricatured as insincere, manipulative, and selfish. To determine the authenticity of the blues experience, one must hear and see raw, unadorned emotion expressed with unpretentiousness and vulnerability. The universality of emotional experiences explains the timeless appeal of this musical folk form.

NOTE

1. W.E.B. Du Bois, *The Souls of Black Folk*, in *Three Negro Classics* (New York: Avon, 1965), 380, 386.

THE BLUES

The blues as a distinctly African American art form and artistic expression of the folk have been treated thoroughly in literature and popular culture. In this essay, former high school teacher and theater critic Michael Lasser offers an abbreviated history of blues music. Notice the connections Lasser makes regarding the southern roots of blues and the relationship between blues and other musical genres—rap, hip hop, gospel, and jazz. While Lasser defines blues as an American art form, he also cites key figures who have made blues the important cultural signifier that it is today: W. C. Handy, George White, Ma Rainey, Bessie Smith, Harold Arlen, Johnny Mercer, and Leadbelly.

MICHAEL LASSER, "SINGIN' THE BLUES" (1996)

From the back-country farms of the Mississippi Valley and the sporting houses of New Orleans, to the twangy rhythms of the Grand Ole Opry and the Manhattan of the Cotton Club and George Gershwin's rhapsody, the blues are everywhere America sings.

Whatever your taste, the fact is that without the blues, there would be no jazz, no gospel, no R&B, no rock 'n' roll, no rap, no Zydeco. Without the blues, we would hardly have American music. What began as a rural folk music of untutored black men and women has become an essential part of American song.

Music historian James Haskins writes, "The blues represented the cries of people who had nothing, who seemed to get nothing no matter how hard they tried, and whose lives seemed hopeless. . . . Such songs were often sung in lively rhythms—like laughing to keep from crying."

Although the human race has always sung songs of despair, the roots of the blues trace back to the slave ships that sailed to the New World from West Africa. The musical traditions of black Africans took root in the deep South, absorbed new influences, and eventually migrated north in the decades following the Civil War.

Soon after they began to arrive in the 17th century, slaves embraced Christianity and its promise of escape from the hardships of daily life. Their early religious songs in America were either "sorrow songs"—the lamentations of an oppressed people—or "shouts"—wild outbursts of religious ecstasy. Both forms of expression eventually influenced the blues.

Soon after the Civil War, freed blacks found jobs in the mines and cotton fields of the South. Others, less fortunate, toiled on prison rock piles and road crews. Their labor produced a body of work songs which sustained them through backbreaking days and expressed the despair they must have felt. One music historian calls these songs the direct "precursors of the blues."

At roughly the same time, new migrants from farms and small towns, who had learned to improvise primitive melodies on banjos and guitars, took their music to the burgeoning cities along the Mississippi. Borrowing from what they heard, blacks in New Orleans began improvising a new kind of personal "sorrow song" on street corners and in saloons. Secular rather than religious, the songs portrayed the troubles of daily life—poverty, injustice. Probably sometime in the 1890s, the songs took shape as the blues, sung over the next decades by people like Huddie Ledbetter, or Leadbelly.

Soon, professional songwriters and performers began to work with this new music. None was more important than a formally trained black cornetist named William Christopher Handy.

W.C. Handy wrote his first blues in 1909 as a campaign song for a Memphis mayoral candidate named Crump. In 1912, he published "Mr. Crump" as "The Memphis Blues."

Some consider "The Memphis Blues" the first blues song, although four years later Handy wrote the most famous of all blues songs, "St. Louis Blues." It is one of the most frequently recorded songs in the history of music, and deservedly so.

Though he based his songs on black folk melodies, Handy was not writing classic blues. He no longer used the characteristic three-line rhymed stanza, and his blues songs soon reached the songwriters of Tin Pan Alley. Once they did, their popularity spread fast and far. During the 1920s, the blues became widely accepted by black *and* white audiences.

Popular composers who had never been further south than Lower Manhattan were soon writing successful blues songs with such titles as "I Ain't Got Nobody," "Squeeze Me," "You Can't Keep a Good Man Down," and "Baby, Won't You Please Come Home." Eventually, the blues even made it to Broadway, in a lavish production number entitled "The Birth of the Blues," as part of George White's Scandals of 1926.

A few years before Handy began to write blues songs, vaudeville singer "Ma" Rainey became known as the "Mother of the Blues." The first of the great female blues singers, Ma gave her black audiences messages of broken dreams and surprisingly explicit sexuality. The "shouts" of slavery days had evolved into a new kind of blues song—boisterous double entendre songs that sang about sexuality with raucous humor and enthusiasm.

But no one sang the blues better than Bessie Smith, known as "The Empress." Blessed with an extraordinarily rich voice and a flamboyant stage manner, she soon became the most famous black singer of the 1920s. When she began to record, she became the first black blues singer discovered by white audiences. The pain Bessie sang about also characterized her own life. In 1937, soon after she began a performing tour, her car crashed into a truck. Her right arm nearly severed, she lay on a lonely country road for hours before help came; she died soon afterwards.

When you think about the different blues musicians, the blues become even more an American story. One set of white collaborators, Harold Arlen and Johnny Mercer, is especially interesting. Russian-born composer Arlen was the son of a cantor. Lyricist Mercer grew up in Savannah, Ga., and attended private school as a boy. Both men absorbed the rhythms of jazz and the blues as teenagers and beginning musicians.

Arlen is best known as the writer of the songs for the movie, "The Wizard of Oz." Mercer is widely regarded as the finest lyricist our popular music produced. In 1941, they collaborated on what may just be the greatest of all blues songs, "Blues in the Night."

In recent years, Mick Jagger of the Rolling Stones acknowledged the influence of the blues on his singing. Seems like it's a long way from sorrow songs to rock 'n' roll . . . but then again, maybe it's not so far after all.

Each year, during the first weekend in June, blues fans gather at the Chicago Blues Festival, one of the major festivals of blues music in the United States. There, musicians and fans reaffirm the continuing vitality of blues music, celebrating and discovering anew why the blues remain an indispensable part of the history and the future of American music.

Geico Direct, Spring 1996, pp. 32–33.

In this poem, poet and performer Priscilla Hancock Cooper conveys the universality of feeling the blues that emerges from heartache and emotional pain. The contradictions of the blues—that celebrations of love are also acknowledgments of human vulnerabilities—are highlighted in this poem as the narrator initially distances herself from the "lowly" experiences that define the blues, only to be brought to the realization that she too is emotionally and spiritually low as her heart hurts from loss. Compare Nanny's blues with Janie's blues in the novel.

PRISCILLA HANCOCK COOPER, "BLUES SONG" (1993)

the blues was a song
  someone else sang
    who had picked cotton
    or did washing
    or washed windows
    or swept floors
    or couldn't find a way to feed her children.
the blues was a song
  of hard times
    removed from the world of
      college degrees
      and cultural awareness
      and pan-africanism
      and I know who I/you/we
        am-ism
the blues was the song
    of the brother downtown
    who rose at six
    and walked 'til five
    and earned not one penny
    and returned to the corner
      dependent on friends
      to buy the wine
      to drown his sorrows
the blues was the song
  of someone else
  someone older
  someone less wise
  someone un-educated
  someone un-aware
  someone
    other than
      this woman until
        she   loved a man
            lost a child
            left her home
        and   locked herself
            into her world
            humming
              the blues.

Priscilla Hancock Cooper, *Call Me Black Woman*, Louisville, KY: Doris Publications, 1993, pp. 10–11.

TOPICS FOR WRITTEN OR ORAL EXPLORATION: BLUES

1. Compare the lyrics and themes of a Negro spiritual to those of a blues song.

2. Discuss the significance of language simplicity for expressing complex emotions in both spirituals and the blues.

3. Discuss the significance of simple word repetitions in blues songs.

4. Write a blues song.

5. Identify specific moments in *Their Eyes Were Watching God* that constitute blues moments.

6. Discuss the gender component of the blues. Identify leading blues singers and what they sing about. Are women more at risk of getting bad reputations as blues singers than men?

7. Identify Janie's blues in her relationship with Nanny.

8. Identify Janie's blues in her relationship with Logan Killicks.

9. Identify Janie's blues in her relationship with Jody Starks.

10. Identify Janie's blues in her relationship with Tea Cake.

11. To what extent do other characters—Nanny, Logan, and Jody—sing the blues?

12. Look at the lyrics of blues songs by Aretha Franklin, Etta James, Billie Holiday, and Bessie Smith for thematic parallels to Janie's experiences in *Their Eyes Were Watching God*.

13. Have each student locate a blues tune to analyze for the class. Bring the tune to class to play in order to show the connection between the lyrics and the music.

14. View the movie and then locate and analyze the lyrics of Billie Holiday's songs from the 1972 movie *Lady Sings the Blues*, set in New York City in 1936.

15. Read and report on the lives of women blues singers. Compare their biographies or autobiographies to Janie's story.

16. Find instances in the novel that might constitute blues moments: Janie's jealousy, violence, loneliness, disappointment, Tea Cake's singing of the blues and gospel. Consider also general musical references that constitute the novel's lyrical core and presentation.

SUGGESTED READINGS ON BLUES

Albertson, Chris. *Bessie*. New York: Stein and Day, 1974.

Baraka, Imamu Amiri. *Blues People: Negro Music in White America*. New York: W. Morrow, 1963.

Bastin, Bruce. *Red River Blues: The Blues Tradition in the Southeast*. Urbana: University of Illinois Press, 1986.

Bethel, Lorraine. " 'This Infinity of Conscious Pain': Zora Neale Hurston and the Black Female Literary Tradition." In Gloria T. Hull, Patricia Bell Scott, and Barbara Smith, eds., *All the Women Are White, All the Blacks Are Men, But Some of Us Are Brave: Black Women's Studies*. New York: Feminist Press, 1982, pp. 176–188.

"The Blues." In Richard Barksdale and Keneth Kinnamon, eds., *Black Writers of America: A Comprehensive Anthology*. New York: Macmillan, 1972, pp. 460–462.

"The Blues." In Henry Louis Gates Jr. and Nellie Y. McKay, eds., *The Norton Anthology of African American Literature*. New York: W. W. Norton, 1997, pp. 22–36.

"Blues." In Langston Hughes and Arna Bontemps, eds., *Book of Negro Folklore*. New York: Dodd, Mead, 1958, pp. 371–397.

Brown, Sterling. "The Blues as Folk Poetry." In Langston Hughes and Arna Bontemps, eds., *The Book of Negro Poetry*. New York: Dodd, Mead, 1958, pp. 371–386.

Dall, Christine, director. "Wild Women Don't Have the Blues." San Francisco: Resolution Incorporated/California Newsreel, 1989. Video cassette.

Davis, Angela Y. *Blues Legacies and Black Feminism: Gertrude "Ma" Rainey, Bessie Smith, and Billie Holiday*. New York: Pantheon Books, 1998.

Dolan, Maria Helena. "Bessie's Blues." *Southern Voices* (22 February 1996): 13.

Evans, David. *Big Road Blues: Tradition and Creativity in the Folk Blues*. Berkeley: University of California Press, 1982.

Ferri, William R., Jr. *Mississippi Black Folklore: A Research Bibliography and Discography*. Hattiesburg: University and College Press of Mississippi, 1971.

Franklin, Aretha. "Do Right Woman, Do Right Man." *Aretha Franklin: 30 Greatest Hits*. New York: Atlantic Recording, 1985. Sound recording. D202329.

———. "Don't Play That Song." *Aretha Franklin: 30 Greatest Hits*. New York: Atlantic Recording, 1985. Sound recording. D202329.

———. "Dr. Feelgood." *Aretha Franklin: 30 Greatest Hits*. New York: Atlantic Recording, 1985. Sound recording. D202329.

———. "I Never Loved a Man (The Way That I Love You)." *Aretha Franklin: 30 Greatest Hits*. New York: Atlantic Recording, 1985. Sound recording. D202329.

———. "Oh Me Oh My (I'm a Fool for You Baby)." *Aretha Franklin: 30 Greatest Hits*. New York: Atlantic Recording, 1985. Sound recording. D202329.

———. "RESPECT." *Aretha Franklin: 30 Greatest Hits*. New York: Atlantic Recording, 1985. Sound recording. D202329.

———. "Since You've Been Gone." *Aretha Franklin: 30 Greatest Hits*. New York: Atlantic Recording, 1985. Sound recording. D202329.

———. "Until You Come Back to Me." *Aretha Franklin: 30 Greatest Hits*. New York: Atlantic Recording, 1985. Sound recording. D202329.

———. "You Make Me Feel Like a Natural Woman." *Aretha Franklin: 30 Greatest Hits*. New York: Atlantic Recording, 1985. Sound recording. D202329.

———. "You're All I Need to Get By." *Aretha Franklin: 30 Greatest Hits*. New York: Atlantic Recording, 1985. Sound recording. D202329.

Handy, W. C., ed. *Blues: An Anthology/Complete Words and Music of 53 Great Songs*. New York: Da Capo Press, 1985.

Harrison, Daphne Duval. *Black Pearls: Blues Queens of the 1920s*. New Brunswick, NJ: Rutgers University Press, 1988.

James, Etta. "All I Could Do Is Cry." *The Essential Etta James*. Universal City, CA: MCA Records, 1993. Sound recording. D254574.

———. "Anything to Say You're Mine." *The Essential Etta James*. Universal City, CA: MCA Records, 1993. Sound recording. D254574.

———. "At Last." *The Essential Etta James*. Universal City, CA: MCA Records, 1993. Sound recording. D254574.

———. "Do Right Woman, Do Right Man." *The Essential Etta James*. Universal City, CA: MCA Records, 1993. Sound recording. D254574.

———. "I'd Rather Go Blind." *The Essential Etta James*. Universal City, CA: MCA Records, 1993. Sound recording. D254574.

———. "If I Can't Have You." *The Essential Etta James*. Universal City, CA: MCA Records, 1993. Sound recording. D254574.

———. "Miss Pitiful." *The Essential Etta James*. Universal City, CA: MCA Records, 1993. Sound recording. D254574.

———. "Next Door to the Blues." *The Essential Etta James*. Universal City, CA: MCA Records, 1993. Sound recording. D254574.

———. "Prisoner of Love." *The Essential Etta James*. Universal City, CA: MCA Records, 1993. Sound recording. D254574.

————. "Something's Got a Hold on Me." *The Essential Etta James*. Universal City, CA: MCA Records, 1993. Sound recording. D254574.

LaSalle, Denise. "Your Husband Is Cheatin' on Us." *The Blues Is Alright*. Jackson, MS: Malaco Records, 1993. Sound recording. MCD 7430.

Lasser, Michael. "Singin' the Blues." *Geico Direct* (Spring 1996): 32–33.

Moore, Dorothy. "Misty Blue." *The Blues Is Alright*. Jackson, MS: Malaco Records, 1993. Sound recording. MCD 7430.

Palmer, Robert. *Deep Blues*. New York: Penguin, 1982.

Phillips, Esther. "Blow Top Blues." *Confessin' the Blues*. New York: Atlantic Records, 1976. Sound recording. 790670–2.

————. "Confessin' the Blues." *Confessin' the Blues*. New York: Atlantic Records, 1976. Sound recording. 790670–2.

————. "Jelly Jelly Blues." *Confessin' the Blues*. New York: Atlantic Records, 1976. Sound recording. 790670–2.

————. "Long John Blues." *Confessin' the Blues*. New York: Atlantic Records, 1976. Sound recording. 790670–2.

Smith, Bessie. "I Ain't Gonna Play No Second Fiddle." *Bessie Smith: The Collection*. New York: CBS Records, 1989. Sound recording. 44441.

————. "My Sweetie Went Away." *Bessie Smith: The Collection*. New York: CBS Records, 1989. Sound recording. 44441.

————. "Tain't Nobody's Bizness." *Bessie Smith: The Collection*. New York: CBS Records, 1989. Sound recording. 44441.

THEATER AND THEATRICAL PERFORMANCE
IN *THEIR EYES WERE WATCHING GOD*

When the people on the muck are trapped by the hurricane, they forget their petty differences and turn their eyes toward the source of their very existence, a force that controls and actually *is* nature. As the storm rages, the frightened victims stare into darkness, praying for relief and safety. Their humility is matched only by God's display of natural theatrics. With this image and the title, Hurston creates a metaphor of theater and theatrical performance based on actions and witnesses. Indeed, Hurston presents *Their Eyes Were Watching God* as a theatrical performance with the characters alternating roles between performer and audience. Notice instances of characters watching and assessing each other through the opening scene of the porch-sitters gossiping about Janie as she heads back into town in a costume they feel is inappropriate for various reasons. Characters also watch, respond to, and become part of the performance rituals of those on the porch telling stories of the mule, watching Mrs. Tony Robbins perform for Jody Starks at his store, witnessing and encouraging the menfolks to compete for Daisy's attentions. There is even performance involved in Janie's observations of the bees pollinating the trees that she later defines as marriage. Nanny performs for Janie, Janie performs for Nanny by marrying Logan Killicks, Jody performs for all the easily impressed colored folks in his new town, Janie performs for Jody in the role of mayor's wife, and Janie performs mourning rituals upon Jody's death. Such conscious and often calculated performance rituals cease for Janie early in her liberating relationship with Tea Cake. However, when Tea Cake feels the need to show other folks on the muck that he is his own man despite the fact that Janie has more materially than he does, he too performs. One of the final performances occurs in Janie's court trial as characters watch, listen, and testify.

In terms of Hurston's title itself, one should recognize that the novel is really not about Christianity and an affirmation of a Christian god external to human beings. And although there is much biblical language and scriptural imagery to suggest a kind of Christian reading of the novel, the text seems to show the various ways by which human beings define god for themselves. Hurston writes:

> All gods dispense suffering without reason. Otherwise they would not be worshipped. Through indiscriminate suffering men know fear and fear is the most divine emotion. It is the stones for altars and the beginning of wisdom. Half gods are worshipped in wine and flowers. Real gods require blood. (*TEWWG* 216–217)

For some of the characters, god is materialism—forty acres and a mule. For another, god is white folks' physical features. Jody's speech habit, "I, god," signals his self-perception as he comes into the colored town and brings light to the allegedly unenlightened colored folks. For all the characters at the moment of the storm, god is the source of all human existence. For Janie, god is simultaneously the strengthening and the humbling force of romantic love.

The final reading in this chapter offers details of a dance production that retells Hurston's story without words but with the voices of southern blues. The example of dance illustrates the versatility and depth of Hurston's text in terms of its applicability to cross-disciplinary interpretation.

TOPICS FOR WRITTEN OR ORAL EXPLORATION: THEATER

1. Note instances of biblical imagery and biblical language in the novel. Discuss their significance and appropriateness.

2. How is gossiping or talking excessively about someone close to idolatry?

3. Are Hurston's redefinitions of "god" anti-Christian?

4. Locate in the text instances of people watching others perform tasks. What is important about the watching?

5. To what extent can Shakespeare's famous line—"All the world's a stage . . ."—apply to Hurston's text thematically and structurally?

THEIR EYES WERE WATCHING GOD AS DANCE PERFORMANCE

In 1988, Dianne McIntyre directed and choreographed what she terms a "choreodrama" based on Zora Neale Hurston's *Their Eyes Were Watching God*. In the following conversation, McIntyre talks about the power of the novel and her efforts to transform the novel into her own dance vision called *"Their Eyes Were Watching God: A Dance Adventure in Southern Blues."* Original music was by Olu Dara and Butch Morris, with dance company Sounds in Motion, along with the Okra Orchestra. The following conversation between the author and Ms. McIntyre took place on July 14, 1998.

CONVERSATION WITH NEW YORK CHOREOGRAPHER DIANNE McINTYRE (JULY 14, 1998)

LESTER: I've lectured on Zora Neale Hurston's *Their Eyes Were Watching God* with the Alabama Humanities Foundation for well over two years and have mostly focused on black people's talking rituals. That's essentially what this book, *Understanding Zora Neale Hurston's* Their Eyes Were Watching God: *A Student Casebook to Issues, Sources, and Historical Documents* is all about—black self-empowerment and black women's empowerment through talking. I've also talked about the novel as a blues text with a distinctly African American blues aesthetic—survival out of hopelessness and despair—and connected the blues with the Negro spirituals, the folk, and emotion. It was never quite clear to me as a teacher and a literary scholar how you had conceptualized the novel as a dance drama, or "choreodrama." I want readers to know that the novel itself is so rich in yielding so many possibilities of dealing with it.

MCINTYRE: My choreodrama of *Their Eyes Were Watching God* was a very successful piece. The only reason we didn't keep doing it as a choreodrama was that it was technically difficult to mount because it had a set. There are some other pieces I've done as dance that have crossed over into theater. When they cross over into theater we have the support of traditional theater. But we really did *Their Eyes Were Watching God* in the dance world. At the time of *Their Eyes Were Watching God*, I was doing theater but as a choreographer; that was the original impulse for it. Woodie King, producer and director of New Federal Theater at Henry

Dianne McIntyre appears as Janie Crawford in the 1987 production of "*Their Eyes Were Watching God*: A Dance Adventure in Southern Blues (a Choreodrama)," presented by Dance Visions, Incorporated. McIntyre accentuates Janie's celebration of a "common folk" lifestyle of unpretentiousness as she parades unapologetically before the townspeople in overalls and challenges their expectations of how she should dress and live. Photograph by Johan Elbers. Reproduced courtesy of Dianne McIntyre.

Street Settlement in New York City, told me that he felt that modern dance could be more accessible to the public if it was related to something they know in literature. So he told me to find a book that I really loved and to see what I could do with it choreographically, and to use the same title as the book. So I went around a long time trying to avoid *Their Eyes Were Watching God*. I thought it would be too difficult. But I finally came back to it.

LESTER: So Hurston's novel is one of your favorites too?

MCINTYRE: Yeah. It's so complete in itself. Woodie had the idea that what I would do would be an abstraction. But as we started working, we found that the whole story could be told in dance without speaking. These successive pieces that I've done have included words, movement and music. But when we did *Their Eyes* it was like a ballet with totally no talking at all. People understood it whether they knew the novel or not.

LESTER: You went through Janie's life with her three husbands?

MCINTYRE: Yeah. We did the whole thing.

LESTER: How did you create the blues dimension specifically so that the piece was not just a ballet or narrative?

MCINTYRE: It was in the music. The music was written by two composers, Olu Dara and Butch Morris. I wanted them both. I don't know how we afforded it, but it worked out. Olu and Butch were connected historically; they worked together. Olu has the feeling of the music of that time period—the 1920s and 1930s—and that place—the Southeast. He was originally a jazz musician but his roots are in Mississippi. Over the years, he's gone back to the music of his southern roots.

LESTER: So Dara and Morris created original pieces for your piece?

MCINTYRE: Yes. They created the music for it. Butch Morris's music created what I call the intrigue in the piece. Olu's music created the layers and the folk, the feelings, the time and the place.

LESTER: You had characters there as well, the porch-sitters, the town gossips, as well as Janie and her men?

MCINTYRE: Yeah. The gossips section was really great!

LESTER: Sounds to me like taking away the words as you've done, the music further blurs the lines between the religious and the secular. Does that come across in your piece?

MCINTYRE: I don't know.

LESTER: In one sense, the townspeople become the chorus, the choir, and there's always gossip going on in the church and at church gatherings and other related social gatherings.

MCINTYRE: Yeah. If you don't actually hear the words, it can feel like church.

LESTER: And with the centrality of emotion present as well.

MCINTYRE: Yeah. I guess it could be. The production was certainly full of emotion. The first time we did it was in a little tiny loft and with this huge set. People said it was their favorite production because it was like a storefront church or something. It was in the summer and it was hot. So the people were in the heat and were real close to us. They liked that one. We didn't invite the critics for that one because I didn't think it was ready. Then sometime in the future, it was harder to get them [critics] there. That first time would have been ideal.

LESTER: So, critically, it was well received?

MCINTYRE: It was in a way. There was one woman from the *Village Voice* that wrote something terrible about it. I can't remember what it was though. We liked doing it, but we stopped doing it because technically it's not that easy. The set was very heavy. Some other people wanted to do it, another company. Some people in California wanted to take it on. I never got the opportunity to pass it on. We did the whole thing, had the whole band. The music's live. That's what I do all the time. I work with live music.

LESTER: Part of what Hurston is doing goes back to the core of black folks' existence—it's raw, unpretentious. The more consciously intellectual stuff can jump over people's heads sometimes. What you've done with the novel beyond the written text is certainly important.

MCINTYRE: Yes. The reason we called it "an adventure in southern blues" has to do with the fact that we had originally wanted to call it *Their Eyes Were Watching God*. And there was a woman during that period who had the rights to the book for several years. She called me after reading about the project and said we couldn't use that title because of copyright violations. I guess that's when we added the subtitle. That was the original intent, to use the name of the book.

LESTER: Did you as a choreographer write a "script" for this dance project as one might write a script for a narrative or drama?

MCINTYRE: I made some notes, but basically the book was the script. I guess I could have worked with an in-between person who might have written an outline, but the book itself was the script. The idea for the set came from the section of the book where Hurston writes about crayon drawings: "When the people sat around on the porch and passed the pictures of their thoughts for the others to look at and see, it was nice. The fact that the thought pictures were always crayon enlargements of life made it even nicer to listen to" (*TEWWG* 81). From that idea of crayon drawings, we made the set as crayon drawings. Even the mule was in cardboard and drawn with crayons.

LESTER: And that crayon-drawn set further supports the fantasy/dream motif present in the novel's structure, theme, language and general aesthetic.

MCINTYRE: Yes.

TOPICS FOR EXPLORATION: THEATER, DANCE, AND MUSIC

1. Imagine *Their Eyes Were Watching God* as a ballet. Dance out certain key scenes of the novel to blues music selections.

2. Rewrite parts of the novel as a dramatic script and act out short scenes.

3. Make up a contemporary blues tune based on current events. For instance, if President Bill Clinton had a blues song about his impeachment, how would it sound and what would it say?

4. Write a blues song that centers around humor from disappointment or struggle.

5. Imagine your pet singing a blues song. How would it go? What would it say?

6. Act out with preacher and congregation members the novel's mock sermon/eulogy on the deceased mule.

7. Locate passages in the novel when characters sing the blues. With Hurston's words, make up a tune for the words and perform.

8. Read autobiographical accounts of Hurston's life and dramatize the most interesting moments as short skits.

9. View and discuss the American Playhouse dramatic production "Zora Is My Name!," produced by Iris Merlis of KCET in Los Angeles, CA (1990). The teleplay was written by Ann Wallace, and based on the play *Zora Is My Name!* by Ruby Dee. The production is directed by Neema Barnette.

Selected Bibliography

Beilke, Debra. " 'Yowin' and Jawin': Humor and the Performance of Identity in Zora Neale Hurston's *Jonah's Gourd Vine*." *Southern Quarterly: A Journal of Arts in the South* 36 (Spring 1998): 21–33.

Caron, Timothy P. " 'Tell Ole Pharaoh to Let My People Go': Communal Deliverance in Zora Neale Hurston's *Moses, Man of the Mountain*." *Southern Quarterly: A Journal of Arts in the South* 36 (Spring 1998): 47–60.

Crawley, Laura K., and Joseph C. Hickerson. *Zora Neale Hurston: Recordings, Manuscripts, and Ephemera in the Archive of Folk Culture and Other Divisions of the Library of Congress*. Washington, DC: Archive of Folk Culture, American Folklife Center, August 1992.

Eble, Kenneth E. *Zora Neale Hurston*. Boston: Twayne, 1980.

Gates, Henry Louis, Jr. "Zora Neale Hurston and the Speakerly Text." In *The Signifying Monkey: A Theory of African-American Literary Criticism*. New York: Oxford University Press, 1988, pp. 170–216.

Gates, Henry Louis, Jr., and K. A. Appiah, eds. *Zora Neale Hurston: Critical Perspectives Past and Present*. New York: Amistad, 1993.

Grant, Alice Morgan. *Jump at the Sun: Zora Neale Hurston and her Eatonville Roots: A Guide for Teachers*. Eatonville, FL: Association to Preserve the Eatonville Community, 1990.

Hemenway, Robert E. *Zora Neale Hurston: A Literary Biography*. Urbana: University of Illinois Press, 1977.

Holder, Laurence. "Zora." In Woodie King Jr., ed., *New Plays for the Black Theatre*. Chicago: Third World Press, 1989, pp. 137–152.

Holloway, Karla F. C. *The Character of the Word: The Texts of Zora Neale Hurston*. Westport, CT: Greenwood Press, 1987.

Hughes, Langston, and Zora Neale Hurston. *Mule Bone: A Comedy of Negro Life*. New York: HarperPerennial, 1991.

Hurst, Fannie. "Zora Hurston: A Personality Sketch." *Yale University Library Gazette* 35 (July 1960): 17–22.

Hurston, Zora Neale. "Art and Such." In Henry Louis Gates Jr., ed., *Reading Black, Reading Feminist: A Critical Anthology*. New York: Meridian, 1990, pp. 21–26.

———. "Color Struck (A Play in Four Scenes)." In Kathy A. Perkins, ed., *Black Female Playwrights: An Anthology of Plays before 1950*. Bloomington: Indiana University Press, 1989, pp. 89–102.

———. *The Complete Stories*. New York: HarperPerennial, 1995.

———. *Dust Tracks on a Road*. New York: HarperPerennial, 1991.

———. "The First One (A Play in One Act)." In Kathy A. Perkins, ed., *Black Female Playwrights: An Anthology of Plays before 1950*. Bloomington: Indiana University Press, 1989, pp. 80–88.

———. *Jonah's Gourd Vine*. New York: Harper and Row, 1990.

———. *Moses, Man of the Mountain*. New York: HarperPerennial, 1991.

———. *Mules and Men*. New York: Harper and Row, 1990.

———. *Mules and Men*. New York: Caedmon, 1991. Audio cassette.

———. *Tell My Horse: Voodoo and Life in Haiti and Jamaica*. New York: Harper and Row, 1990.

———. *The Sanctified Church: The Folklore Writings of Zora Neale Hurston*. Berkeley, CA: Turtle Island, 1981.

———. *Seraph on the Suwanee*. New York: HarperPerennial, 1991.

———. *Their Eyes Were Watching God*. New York: Harper and Row, 1990.

———. "Three by Zora Neale Hurston: Story, Essay, and Play." *Southern Quarterly: A Journal of Arts in the South* 36 (Spring 1998): 94–102.

Kennedy, Stetson. "Postscript: The Mark of Zora." In Henry Louis Gates Jr., ed., *Reading Black, Reading Feminist: A Critical Anthology*. New York: Meridian, 1990, pp. 27–29.

Lancaster, Lillian. *Suggestions for Incorporating the Writings of Zora Neale Hurston in the English IIIS, III, and IIIH Curriculum*. Eatonville, FL: Association to Preserve the Eatonville Community, 1989. Teacher's guide.

Lester, Neal A. "Sounds of Silent Performances: Homoeroticism in Zora Neale Hurston's 'Story in Harlem Slang: Jelly's Tale.'" *Southern*

Quarterly: A Journal of Arts in the South 36 (Spring 1998): 10–20.

Lillios, Anna, guest ed. "Special Feature: Zora Neale Hurston." *Southern Quarterly: A Journal of Arts in the South* 36 (Spring 1998).

———. " 'The Monstrous Beast': The Hurricane in Zora Neale Hurston's *Their Eyes Were Watching God.*" *Southern Quarterly: A Journal of Arts in the South* 36 (Spring 1998): 89–93.

Lowe, John. " 'Seeing Beyond Seeing': Zora Neale Hurston's Religion(s)." *Southern Quarterly: A Journal of Arts in the South* 36 (Spring 1998): 77–78.

Plant, Deborah C. *Every Tub Must Sit on Its Own Bottom: The Philosophy and Politics of Zora Neale Hurston.* Urbana: University of Illinois Press, 1995.

Pratt, Theodore. "Zora Neale Hurston: Florida's First Distinguished Author." *Negro Digest* (February 1962): 52–56.

Sharp, Patricia. "*Their Eyes Were Watching God.*" In Frank N. Magill, ed., *Masterpieces of African-American Literature: Descriptions, Analyses, Characters, Plots, Themes, Critical Evaluations, and Significance of Major Works of Fiction, Nonfiction, Drama and Poetry.* New York: HarperCollins, 1992, pp. 569–572.

Smith, Barbara. "Sexual Politics and the Fiction of Zora Neale Hurston." *Radical Teacher* 8 (May 1978): 26–30.

Speisman, Barbara. "From 'Spears' to *The Great Day*: Zora Neale Hurston's Vision of a Real Negro Theater." *Southern Quarterly: A Journal of Arts in the South* 36 (Spring 1998): 34–46.

Walker, Alice, ed. *I Love Myself When I Am Laughing . . . and Then Again When I Am Looking Mean and Impressive: A Zora Neale Hurston Reader.* New York: Feminist Press, 1979.

———. "Looking for Zora." In *In Search of Our Mothers' Gardens: Womanist Prose.* San Diego: Harcourt Brace Jovanovich, 1983, pp. 93–116.

———. "Zora Neale Hurston: A Cautionary Tale and a Partisan View." In *In Search of Our Mothers' Gardens: Womanist Prose.* San Diego: Harcourt Brace, 1983, pp. 83–92.

Washington, Mary Helen. "Zora Neale Hurston's Work: The Black Woman's Search for Identity." *Black World* 21 (August 1972): 68–75.

Index

About the Author

NEAL A. LESTER is Professor of English at Arizona State University, where he teaches African American literature. He is the author of *Ntozake Shange: A Critical Study of the Plays* (1995), and has published on Alice Walker, Zora Neale Hurston, and Lonne Elder.